PERFECT FOR
TEACHERS OF GRADES
6-8

Teach Terrific WRITING

Gary Robert Muschla

McGraw·Hill

New York   Chicago   San Francisco   Lisbon   London   Madrid   Mexico City
Milan   New Delhi   San Juan   Seoul   Singapore   Sydney   Toronto

1 2 3 4 5 6 7 8 9 10 11 12 13 14 15   QPD/QPD   0 9 8 7 6

ISBN-13: 978-0-07-146317-1
ISBN-10:   0-07-146317-8

Library of Congress Control Number: 2006924892

Interior design by Nick Panos

McGraw-Hill books are available at special quantity discounts to use as premiums and sales promotions, or for use in corporate training programs. For more information, please write to the Director of Special Sales, Professional Publishing, McGraw-Hill, Two Penn Plaza, New York, NY 10121-2298. Or contact your local bookstore.

This book is printed on acid-free paper.

Contents

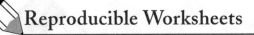

Reproducible Worksheets

Personally Speaking

Friends

School

Out and About

At Your Leisure

Sports and Play

Part 2
Writing the Draft

113

Part 3
Revision

153

Reproducible Worksheets

Part 4
Proofreading

Reproducible Worksheets

About This Book

Learning to write is a challenging, multiskilled process. Students must learn how to identify, analyze, and develop ideas. They must learn how to compose sentences, build paragraphs, and express ideas within the standards of written English. They must discover their "voice" and learn how to say precisely what they want to say with fluency, clarity, and energy.

Teach Terrific Writing, Grades 6–8 can be a valuable resource as you guide your students through this process. The teaching suggestions, exercises, and reproducible worksheets in this book will enable you to provide your students with meaningful writing assignments and activities. Your students will learn how to find and focus ideas for writing; how to write a draft; how to revise their writing; and how to proofread their work. This book, which is based on the stages of the writing process, will give students the practice they need to acquire the skills for effective composition and to grow as young writers.

Helping your students learn to write is a difficult task. It is my hope that you will find this book useful in that demanding and rewarding challenge.

How to Use This Book

*T*each *Terrific Writing, Grades 6–8* is divided into four parts that concentrate on writing skills, from developing ideas to proofreading, and provide teaching suggestions, exercises, and reproducible worksheets. There is an answer key for the worksheets at the end of the book.

Part 1 "Finding and Developing Ideas for Writing" begins with the understanding that solid ideas are the backbone of good writing. Although ideas are all around, young writers need to learn how to identify and develop ideas for their writing. This part of the book includes information on idea development, teaching suggestions, six exercises, and a hundred reproducible worksheets designed to help students develop material for writing. The worksheets are broken down into seven sections: "Personally Speaking," "Friends," "School," "Out and About," "At Your Leisure," "Sports and Play," and "Weird, Strange, and Unbelievable." Each worksheet, which serves as a prewriting activity, offers students a topic and guidelines they can use to explore and develop the topic.

Part 2 "Writing the Draft" focuses on skills that help students to write with competence and confidence. Along with teaching suggestions and information on the characteristics of good writing, fifteen exercises and twenty-two reproducible worksheets address topics such as using proper sentence structure; combining and varying sentences; constructing paragraphs; using active constructions, strong verbs, and effective transitions; and choosing a point of view.

Part 3 "Revision" focuses on skills and methods necessary for effective revision. Teaching suggestions, three exercises, a reproducible list of guidelines for revision, and twenty-five reproducible worksheets are included. Worksheets, which include both fiction and nonfiction, show students the types of weak composition that can slip into their own writing. Students are required to identify and revise the weaknesses on the worksheets.

Part 4 "Proofreading" examines the skills and methods necessary for effective proofreading. Teaching suggestions, three exercises, a reproducible list of guidelines for proofreading, and twenty-five reproducible worksheets are included in this part of the book. The worksheets, both fiction and nonfiction, present students with the errors in mechanics they will undoubtedly find in their own writing. As students find and correct the errors on the worksheets, they will gain the critical skills necessary for proofreading their own work.

Answer Key includes solutions for the worksheets. In cases where answers vary (for example, revision), possible answers are provided.

The background material, teaching suggestions, exercises, and reproducible worksheets throughout this book are designed to make your teaching easier. Each worksheet stands alone, can be used with students of varying abilities, and is set up in a clear, easy-to-follow format. The worksheets can serve as the basis of your writing program, you may use them to supplement the lessons of your language arts instruction, or you may use them as reviews for material previously taught or as extra-credit assignments. You can even use them with substitute plans. Use the worksheets in whatever manner is most beneficial to your students.

The reproducible worksheets and exercises throughout this book offer nearly two hundred separate activities. They will provide your students with a rich variety of writing experiences and help them gain a better understanding of the writing process.

PART 1

Finding and Developing Ideas for Writing

Good writing begins with a good idea. Without an interesting idea, even the most skillful writing will result in an unremarkable piece. At best, the reader will plod through such a piece, hoping to find something of value; at worst, he will quickly conclude there is nothing of value and put the piece aside.

Aware of the importance of ideas, professional authors spend significant effort and time identifying, developing, researching, analyzing, and organizing ideas before they begin writing. They understand that if they start writing with fuzzy, unclear ideas, they will write with little focus or direction. Instead of writing with purpose and efficiency, they will be writing with confusion and frustration.

This is why it is essential that your students learn how to discover and develop ideas for writing. Fresh ideas are the raw materials of which the foundation for effective expression is built.

Discovering Ideas

Just about every student has numerous ideas that can be the foundation of solid writing. Certainly most middle school students have much to say about almost everything, although they may not know how to find ideas to write about. They may not recognize how ideas are interrelated and how an idea can be expanded and refined—and sometimes entirely transformed—into new ideas that become interesting pieces.

To help your students discover ideas for writing, you need to make them realize that they have a reservoir of ideas within themselves. Through reflection, imagination, and diligence, students can find much to write about. The starting point is personal experience.

Personal Experience: The Source

The seed of every idea takes root in the rich soil of personal experience. From that seed, the idea grows, branches, and, with the right care and nourishment, blossoms and blooms. Not only our direct experiences, but our dreams, our musings, things we hear about or learn, and everything that we experience can be the substance of which an idea can be built.

Following are some examples of personal experiences that can generate ideas.

- A nightmare can provide the preliminary idea for a horror story.
- Practicing for a piano recital can lead to an article about the sacrifice necessary for achievement.
- Seeing a flyer about a lost dog can generate a story about a missing puppy.
- Learning about the Amazon Basin can inspire an essay about the importance of the rain forests.
- Hearing about a big storm can remind a person about a major storm she experienced and lead to a narrative about survival.
- A friend's moving away can be the motivation for written reflection about friendship.

Children have countless experiences that can serve as initial ideas for writing. They simply need to be shown how to access their wealth of experience.

Exercise 1.1 Peering into Personal Experience

Explain to your students that their personal experiences—all the things they have ever done, seen, read, or heard about—can lead to ideas they can use for writing. They must learn how to identify these ideas within their memories.

Write one of the following topics, or a topic of your own, on an overhead projector or the board:

- Meaningful Things
- Friends
- Interests and Hobbies
- Things I Enjoy
- Things That Annoy Me

Ask your students to volunteer examples that can be included under the topic, then write their suggestions beneath the topic. For example, under "Interests and Hobbies," students might suggest examples such as reading, skateboarding, soccer, camping, model building, music, dance—obviously, the list can get quite extensive.

After writing several examples, discuss how each can lead to an idea for writing. Here are some possibilities:

- For reading—a review of a favorite book
- For skateboarding—a description of some of the techniques necessary for "extreme" skateboarding
- For camping—a narrative about a fun camping trip
- For music—an article about a concert, or a favorite singer or group

Depending on your class, you might want to offer some of the other topics for additional examples and reinforcement. Or you might ask students to volunteer some topics and explore ideas that arise from their suggestions.

Emphasize that everyone has personal experiences that can be used to find ideas for writing. Sometimes a personal experience can be developed directly into a topic. Sometimes it can be a spark, igniting the imagination to develop other ideas. Always it is a source of ideas.

The Benefits of Keeping a Journal

An excellent method for tapping into personal experience is to regularly write in a journal. A writing journal is a place where students can express their thoughts and feelings on meaningful topics and issues. In time, a journal can become a warehouse of writing ideas ranging from whimsical musings to the deepest emotions and concerns.

Because the writing in journals tends to be personal and reflective as students explore ideas, I do not recommend that journals be corrected or graded. When journals are graded, students are less willing to experiment with ideas and different forms of writing, and tend to write what they feel the teacher wants to see or what they believe will result in a good grade. This undermines the purpose of the journal, which should be a safe haven, a place a writer can write without concern for convention or form. For some students, their greatest growth as young writers first emerges in their journals.

Although you will find that many students will want to share their journals with you and their friends, student journals should be private unless you explain in advance that you will periodically read them. If you read journals, feel free to write comments, offer suggestions, pose questions to stimulate thinking, or simply share your thoughts. Students will appreciate the feedback.

Do not be surprised if some of your students write notes to you in their journals. It is not uncommon for journals to become a medium through which students and teachers share a dialogue about writing.

Writing journals need not be lavish to be purposeful. A composition book or spiral notebook is sufficient. Some students like to keep their journals on their computers and e-mail some of their writing to their teachers. In whichever form students keep their journals, suggest that they date all entries, because dates provide a time reference that will help students to follow their progress as writers. Also suggest that students review their journals periodically to find ideas for writing.

The Benefits of Reading

Reading is yet another way to tap into personal experience in search of ideas. Reading can present us with new ideas, add information to old ideas, and stimulate reflection on ideas. Reading expands our world and experiences.

The benefits of reading for writing go far beyond expanding our world and experiences, however. Reading also introduces young writers to various forms of writing, idea development, and writing techniques. It is no coincidence that virtually all writers are readers.

Reading should play a prominent role in your classroom in support of writing. You should encourage reading, provide time for it, and make a variety of reading materials available for your students. Reading with and to your students can demonstrate your pleasure in reading and be a powerful model to students.

When you come across an example of exceptional writing in a story, article, or book, point it out to your students. Discuss why the example is exceptional. Note how it adds to the piece in a way only it can. Seeing examples of strong writing in the materials they read helps students to recognize superior expression.

It is through reading that students learn to recognize good writing. Reading, without question, helps students to become better writers.

Seeing Life Through the Eyes of a Writer

Most writers view the world with a sharp, critical eye. They see, they contemplate, and they ask themselves "What if . . . ?" To help your students see the world through the eyes of a writer, encourage them to be both observers and interpreters of life. Encourage them to be inquisitive, curious, and open to new ideas. Encourage them to step outside themselves and to look at things from the perspectives of others.

Offer this example: Ask your students to imagine how their school would appear to a new student from another state. What would be the most striking feature about the school? Would the student feel lost? Out of place? Afraid or anxious? Why might a new student feel this way? Go one step further. Ask your students how their school would seem to a new student from another country who does not speak English. Considering situations and issues from another's point of view can enhance understanding and broaden perspective. It also can lead to new ideas.

Along with viewing things from different perspectives, tell your students to always look for details, using their senses of sight, hearing, touch, taste, and smell. Explain that by paying close attention to their surroundings they can sharpen their powers of observation and learn to see what others overlook.

Offer this example. Ask your students to imagine they are standing in their yard or a park. What do they see? Trees? What kinds of trees? Big? Small? Evergreen or deciduous? Are the leaves green, or are they painted with the colors of autumn? What about animals? Do they see any birds? What kinds? Sparrows? Robins? Crows? Maybe they see a gray squirrel scampering along a branch. What do they hear? The rustle of leaves? The songs of birds? The barking of a dog in the distance? What does the air smell like? Clean? Fresh? Full of the scent of flowers? If the day is windy, how does the wind feel against their face? Against their body? Is it so strong that it pushes them backward? Is the wind cold? Warm? Humid? What about touch? Maybe the ground is soggy beneath their feet because of the previous night's heavy rain. Or perhaps it is hard because it has not rained in days. What about taste? Maybe they are chewing spearmint-flavored gum (sugarless, of course) that makes their mouth feel fresh. Encourage your students to experience the world through their senses. Awareness of details sharpens perspectives and adds to the images that make up ideas.

Exercise 1.2 Seeing the Details

Instruct your students to select a corner or a part of the classroom. (You might prefer to have students do this exercise at home. In that case, instruct them to select a part of a room at home.) While sitting in their seats, they are to list as many details as they can about this part of the room. Tell them to use as many of their senses as possible, though especially sight and hearing. After they are done, have students share some of the details they found. Emphasize that sharp, clear details make ideas come alive.

Seeing through the eyes of a writer broadens the world, enabling a person to become aware of not just the most prominent features of things but the smallest details as well. This is a valuable skill for students that extends well beyond writing and into all aspects of life.

Focusing Ideas

Once general ideas have been explored, they must be focused. Focusing an idea narrows it down so that the writer can concentrate on a specific angle. This is essential for further development.

Consider the topic *studying*. This is broad and unfocused. Does the topic mean studying in general? Or studying for tests? Or studying a particular subject? The topic does not offer much direction. However, the topic *how to study for math tests* is focused and serves as a clear guide for the writer to develop the piece.

5

Finding and Developing Ideas for Writing

A focused topic not only provides a writer with direction, but also enables a writer to channel her attention and remain on topic. Focused topics are more likely to result in unified pieces in which all the material of the piece relates to a whole.

Exercise 1.3 Narrowing Ideas Down

Write one of the following general topics, or a similar topic of your choosing, on an overhead projector or the board:

- Fun Activities
- Pets
- Family

Explain to your students that these are broad topics that lack focus for writing. Start with one of the topics and ask your students to offer focused examples for it. Write their suggestions beneath the topic. You may find it beneficial to do a second, or perhaps third topic for reinforcement.

Here is an example: Fun activities . . . snowboarding . . . snowboarding at a ski lodge . . . the best snowboarding day of my life. Note how the topics become more focused.

Here is another example: Pets . . . dogs and cats . . . dogs . . . beagles . . . my beagle . . . finding Sleuth. Note how the general topics proceed to a specific one, which refers to the time Sleuth, the beagle, got lost.

Now here is an example using family: Family . . . my mother, father, younger brother . . . younger brother getting into mischief . . . the time my brother drew pictures on his bedroom walls. Notice how the general topics become more focused, leading to the younger brother's budding artistic skills.

These are simple examples, but they will effectively illustrate for students how to focus ideas. It should also become apparent to them that a focused idea is easier to write about because the details are more specific than the details of a general idea.

Developing Ideas

Seldom do ideas for writing burst into a writer's consciousness in complete form. In most cases, ideas are discovered and then must be explored, analyzed, and developed. Through the process of development, ideas may be expanded, refined, or even rejected, only to be resurrected again in new forms. Sometimes an initial idea gives rise to new ideas that then become the focal point of writing. Although developing ideas is hard work, there are steps you can take to make the process easier for your students. These steps include establishing a classroom that welcomes new ideas, posing questions to aid development, identifying relationships, brainstorming, and researching.

Perhaps most important, you must establish a classroom atmosphere in which an appreciation of ideas is fostered and supported. Your classroom should be a place where students are comfortable to share their ideas without fear of mockery or sarcasm.

While criticism is necessary to the evaluation of ideas, it should be positive and constructive. Feelings and opinions in the classroom should always be respected, and ethnicities must be accepted. Students should feel safe in your classroom and at ease in pursuing the development of ideas, confident that their ideas will not be ridiculed.

One of the best strategies for developing ideas is to consider the five *W*s and *How: Who? What? Where? When? Why? How?* Although each of these questions may not be applicable to every idea, they are useful for most.

Exercise 1.4 Using the Five *W*s and *How* to Develop Ideas

Using an overhead projector or the board, write "Lost Gym Bag" as a basic idea for a story. Ask your students how they might build a story from this initial idea. Walk them through the developmental process by writing the following:

- **What?** A gym bag is lost.
- **When?** When was it last seen?
- **Where?** Where was it last seen?
- **Who?** Who are the people in this story? Might one of them have taken the gym bag?
- **Why?** Why was the gym bag lost? Was it simply misplaced? Was it stolen? If yes, why would someone steal it?
- **How?** How was it found? Or perhaps it was not found. In that case, how was the fruitless search conducted?

Explain to your students that using these questions will help them to expand their initial idea and build it into an article or story. Note that the answers to each question lead naturally into more ideas and potentially more questions. Thus, the questions serve as a blueprint that guides writers to building a story.

Another strategy for developing ideas is to look for relationships. Explain to your students that nothing exists in isolation. Relationships may not be apparent at first, but everything is connected in some way to something else.

Offer this example. A honeybee visits a flower and takes some of its nectar. The bee returns to the hive, where the nectar is used to make honey. However, while the bee is on the flower, pollen necessary for plants to reproduce clings to the bee's body. As the bee visits other flowers, some of the pollen rubs off, making the plant's reproduction possible. This relationship is vital to both honeybees and flowers. Mature flowers, however, are important not only for honeybees. They may serve as food for rabbits or deer, be a hiding place for small animals, or simply beautify the countryside or someone's garden. Encouraging your students to recognize relationships between both living and nonliving things is a skill that can serve them well in whatever they do.

To reinforce this concept, point out and discuss relationships in the various subjects in your class whenever you can. Relationships can be complex, but basic ones are easy for students to grasp—for example, cause and effect (studying leads to better grades), interdependence (animals breathe oxygen and exhale carbon dioxide as a by-product, and plants absorb carbon dioxide and release oxygen as a by-product), and parts to wholes (our solar system is a part of the Milky Way galaxy, which is a part of the universe). Make highlighting the connections between things a priority in your classroom, and in time your students will learn to look for and recognize relationships.

Brainstorming is another strategy students can use to develop ideas for writing. A mental exercise in which a person writes down as many ideas as he can about a topic, brainstorming can be a powerful method in the development of ideas. Explain to your students that the purpose of brainstorming is to write as many related ideas about a topic as quickly as possible. They should not pause to analyze ideas during brainstorming, because that only slows the generation of ideas. Evaluation may be done later. Brainstorming is a fast and furious exercise, the purpose of which is to discover and expand ideas.

Exercise 1.5 Brainstorming and Word Webs

Explain to your students that creating a *word web* can help them identify, expand, and develop ideas for writing. On an overhead projector or the board, write the topic "School Lunchroom" in the middle of the page. (If you prefer, you might ask students to suggest a topic. Using a topic students provide assures them that the topic is genuine and not one you picked simply because it works for the activity.)

Ask students to volunteer ideas related to the school lunchroom. They might suggest ideas such as the following: noisy, a break from classes, mystery food, seeing friends, talking with friends, downtime, not enough time to eat, food fights (hopefully not!), and so on. As they offer ideas, write them down. Use a line to connect ideas that stem from other ideas. Write quickly and do not pause to discuss ideas now. Remind students that the goal of brainstorming is to uncover as many related ideas as possible, thereby expanding the original idea.

When you are done, review the ideas the class generated. Explain that some of the ideas on the word web will probably not be used in writing, but others will. Sometimes a web will lead to an entirely new idea that may then lead to a new web and more new ideas for writing.

Although I do not demand that students complete word webs for the development of their ideas, I suggest they do. Brainstormed word webs can help students flesh out and expand initial ideas in a nonthreatening manner that yields fresh possibilities for writing.

Researching is yet another way students can develop ideas for writing. Along with traditional print sources, the Internet and electronic databases provide writers with broad resources for finding information on countless topics. Before the development of the Internet, writers often had to conduct extensive research in order to find information on some topics. Even then, they might not be able to find what they needed. Today, writers often find too much information.

Although you should encourage your students to use the Internet for research when developing writing topics, you should also provide them with guidelines that can help them find what they need. Most important, students need to understand that anyone can post information on the World Wide Web, so not all of the information students will find will be valid or useful. To minimize the chances of finding invalid data or winding up on undesirable sites, caution your students to conduct research on reputable sites, which include the sites of government agencies, major organizations, and universities. Fortunately, many of the best sites often appear near the beginning of the list that results from a search.

To facilitate searching on the Internet, instruct your students to use specific key terms. Most search engines have become so sophisticated that key terms direct the researchers to sites that they will find useful. Certainly for students in sixth through eighth grades, the terms they would use for looking up information in an encyclopedia or other reference book will yield accurate results with most Internet search engines. Having a focused topic will provide students with guidance to keep on track during research, and can help keep them from becoming mired in huge amounts of irrelevant information.

Organizing Ideas

In their enthusiasm (some teachers would call this "rush") to complete their writing, many students want to take their ideas and begin writing immediately. The result is almost always the same: the aspiring writers finish pieces that are so disorganized and require so much revision that they do not know how or where to start to make improvements. Consequently, they do not do much revision, become dissatisfied with their work, and soon become convinced that they are poor writers.

Providing your students with simple techniques for organization will help them to clarify and order their ideas, which makes writing any piece easier. Although a detailed outline is needed for some writing, such as research reports, most of your students' writing will be well served by the basic structure of opening, body, and closing. Convincing students of the need for organization is not easy, but if you keep emphasizing the necessity of a practical plan for writing, your students will eventually learn and employ the basics of organization.

Exercise 1.6 Basic Organization for Nonfiction

Using an overhead projector or the board, write this simple form for structure. Discuss the parts with your students.

- **Opening.** One or two paragraphs
- **Body.** One, two, three, or more paragraphs
- **Closing.** One paragraph

It may help to write this form on poster paper and leave it on display in the room. Encourage students to refer to the form regularly during writing.

Explain the three parts of basic structure. The opening should introduce the topic and the problem or situation the writing is about. The body provides information on the topic, including examples and details. Depending on the topic, the body may be one paragraph, several paragraphs, or several pages long. The closing includes a final point related to the main idea or a brief summary of the main idea expressed in the body.

Illustrate this form using an article from your students' reading program, social studies book, or science text. It is best to use an article for this activity, as the structure for fiction may not be as clear.

Ask students to identify the opening of the article; then the body, including the paragraphs that make it up; and finally the closing. Note that most nonfiction follows this format. Urge students to look for this form in the articles they read.

Helping Students Who Have Trouble Finding Ideas

Despite possessing many experiences that can be the seeds for ideas for writing, some students, through lack of motivation, weak skills, or poor confidence, find it difficult to identify and develop sound ideas. These students require more guidance from you than others.

For students you perceive as lacking motivation, work with them to find ideas that they consider to be interesting. I remember a student who did not like to write, but he liked activities such as dirt-bike racing and helping his father repair cars. Suggesting that he write about these kinds of topics stimulated a desire to share his knowledge of these subjects with others. During that year I learned an awful lot about dirt bikes, but the student wrote consistently and his skills improved significantly.

For students who possess weak skills, you should offer guidance in finding and developing ideas. Once they have identified an idea for writing, go on to the five *W*s and *How* with them. Make sure they answer each question about their topic with specifics, then help them organize their ideas. Having ideas formulated before writing makes the process smoother. You should also identify the writing weaknesses of these students and work with them to strengthen their skills.

For students who have poor confidence, talk with them and try to draw them out. Perhaps they are afraid that people might criticize their writing; or they may be concerned that they have nothing important to say. Assure these students that their ideas are as important as anyone else's. Show interest in what they have to say. Offer genuine praise, for example, "You did a nice job of describing that park," or "I could almost feel the rain pounding down on me." Explain that they should strive to develop their ideas fully and express them clearly.

For most students, offering them latitude in developing ideas fosters a sense of ownership in their writing. While assigning a general topic for writing, encourage them to develop their ideas and express their thoughts as they wish. The worksheets at the end of this section provide students with assignments in which they have the freedom to develop their ideas in ways meaningful for them. This is an environment in which writing can thrive.

Reproducible Worksheets

The following reproducible worksheets can help you to develop your students' basic writing skills. The one hundred worksheets are divided into seven parts:

- Personally Speaking
- Friends
- School
- Out and About
- At Your Leisure
- Sports and Play
- Weird, Strange, and Unbelievable

The themes of the worksheets in each category are loosely based on the title of the category. For example, the worksheets contained in "Personally Speaking" focus on the author in some way. The worksheets in "Sports and Play" focus on sports or some type of playful activity.

While most of the worksheets are to be developed as articles, narratives, or persuasive pieces, several fiction topics are included throughout the categories, with the most fiction appearing in the final category, "Weird, Strange, and Unbelievable." Select the worksheets that you feel will best serve the needs of your students.

Intended to be a prewriting activity, each worksheet is designed to help students conceive ideas for writing on a topic. Most of the topics tie into the experiences of students, making it easier for them to generate material for writing. Moreover, because the topics are general, students have much freedom to develop their ideas. For example, with Worksheet 1.4, "Future Gazing," students are given the general idea of considering what they might be like in the future. They can pick a time a year from now, a few years from now, or many years from now. Answering the questions on the worksheet will stimulate the imaginations of students and present possibilities for writing. From that point, each student can develop the piece in his own way. For example, he may expand the material through brainstorming and word webs. In some cases, to fully develop his ideas, a student may find it helpful to conduct research via print sources or the Internet.

When assigning any of the worksheets, make sure that your students understand what they are to write about. Also make sure they understand terms such as *article*, *narrative*, and *persuasive piece*, as well as terms for fiction including *characters*, *setting*, *description*, *plot*, *action*, *theme*, and *climax*.

Explain to your students that they are to complete the worksheet, using the back of the sheet or an extra sheet of paper if they need more space to answer the questions. Depending on your class, you may want to discuss the questions and offer some suggestions for development. After completing the worksheet, encourage your students to expand their ideas and add more details if necessary. Emphasize that the worksheets are guides. Students may find that not all the information they supply in response to the questions on the worksheets will wind up in their writing, and that sometimes information not related to the questions will. Suggest that they may choose a new title that more accurately reflects their writing. Realizing that ideas can be developed in a variety of ways is essential for idea development to flourish. Encourage your students to organize their ideas before writing and to follow a basic plan of opening, body, and closing.

The purpose of any prewriting activity is to engage the writer's mind with the writing to be done. Once the process is begun, the only limits are the writer's imagination and enthusiasm.

1.1 An Autobiographical Sketch

Directions: An *autobiography* is a true story that a person writes about himself or herself. An *autobiographical sketch* is a short autobiography. Think about your life. Answer the questions and write an autobiographical sketch. Be sure to include an opening, body, and closing in your writing. Support your ideas with details and examples.

1. When and where were you born? _____

2. Describe your physical traits. (Include such qualities as age, height, color of eyes, hair, and so on.) _____

   _____

   _____

3. Describe your personality. _____

   _____

   _____

   _____

4. Name three things you like and why you like them. _____

   _____

   _____

   _____

5. Name three things you dislike and why you dislike them. _____

   _____

   _____

   _____

6. If you had to describe yourself in one word, what would that word be? Explain why this word describes you best. _____

   _____

   _____

1.2 Family Matters

Directions: Think about your family. What makes it special and different from any other family? Answer the questions and write an article about your family. Be sure to include an opening, body, and closing in your writing. Support your ideas with details and examples.

1. Who are the members of your family? _____

   _____

2. Describe the members of your family. (Include physical traits and

   personalities.) _____

   _____

   _____

   _____

   _____

   _____

3. Explain how your family is special. _____

   _____

   _____

   _____

   _____

4. What do you feel is the best thing about your family? Explain. _____

   _____

   _____

   _____

   _____

   _____

1.3 My Pet and Me

Directions: Think about a pet. (If you do not have a pet, imagine that you can have any pet you wish.) Answer the following questions and write an article about your pet. Remember to include an opening, body, and closing in your writing. Support your ideas with details and examples.

1. What kind of pet do you have? _____

2. What is its name? _____

3. Describe your pet's appearance. _____

_____

_____

4. Describe how your pet behaves. _____

_____

_____

_____

5. Describe your pet's favorite place in your home. _____

_____

6. Describe the things your pet likes to do most. _____

_____

7. How do you help care for your pet? _____

_____

_____

_____

1.4 Future Gazing

Directions: Pick a time in the future. This time could be a year from now, a few years from now, or many years from now. Gaze into the future and imagine yourself in that time. Answer the questions and write about yourself in this time period. Be sure to include an opening, body, and closing in your writing. Support your ideas with details and examples.

1. What is the year and where will you be living? _____

2. Describe yourself in the future. In what ways will you have changed? In what ways will you be the same? _____

_____

_____

_____

3. What will you be doing? (For example, will you still be going to school? Will you have a job? What kind?) _____

_____

_____

4. Describe your family and friends. _____

_____

_____

_____

5. Describe a problem you face in the future. _____

_____

6. Describe some good things in the future. _____

_____

_____

1.5 Listen Up!

Directions: Think of a time you offered advice to someone—perhaps a friend, sibling, or even your parents. Maybe a friend asked for advice on how to babysit for a neighbor, or your mom needed your help to fix a computer glitch. Answer the questions and write an article explaining the advice you offered. Be sure to use an opening, body, and closing in your writing. Support your ideas with details and examples.

1. To whom did you offer advice? _____

2. What problem did this person have? _____

_____

_____

3. Why were you able to offer advice on this subject? _____

_____

_____

4. What advice did you offer? _____

_____

_____

_____

_____

5. Did the person to whom you offered advice take your advice? If yes, did
   your advice help him or her to solve the problem? Explain how. If the
   person did not take your advice, explain why. _____

_____

_____

_____

1.6 Lessons

Directions: Think of a time you learned an important lesson. Answer the questions and write a narrative about this experience and what you learned. Remember to include an opening, body, and closing in your writing. Support your ideas with details and examples.

1. What is the subject you are writing about? _____

2. When and where did this happen? _____

3. Who was with you? _____

4. Describe what happened. _____

_____

_____

_____

_____

_____

5. What lesson did you learn? _____

_____

_____

_____

6. Did learning this lesson change you in some way? If yes, how? If not, why

   not? _____

_____

_____

_____

1.7 Ambition

Directions: Think of your ambitions. What do you most want to achieve? Answer the questions and write an article about your greatest ambition. Be sure to include an opening, body, and closing in your writing. Support your ideas with details and examples.

1. What is your greatest ambition? _____

_____

2. Why do you want to achieve this? _____

_____

_____

3. What must you do to achieve your ambition? _____

_____

_____

_____

_____

4. Describe any obstacles that might stop you from achieving your ambition
   and how you will overcome them. _____

_____

_____

_____

5. Do you expect to achieve this ambition one day? Explain. _____

_____

_____

_____

Personally Speaking

1.8 Happy Holidays

Directions: Think about all the holidays you enjoy and decide which one you like best. Answer the questions and write an article about your favorite holiday. Be sure to include an opening, body, and closing in your writing. Support your ideas with details and examples.

1. What are some holidays you enjoy? _____
_____

2. Which one is your favorite? Why? _____
_____
_____
_____

3. With whom do you celebrate this holiday? _____
_____

4. Describe how you celebrate this holiday. _____
_____
_____
_____
_____

5. If you could make this holiday even better, how would you do it?
_____
_____
_____
_____

1.9 Time for a Hero

Directions: Think about a person you consider to be a hero. This person might have lived in the past, or might be living now. Answer the questions and write an article about your hero. Be sure to include an opening, body, and closing in your writing. Support your ideas with details and examples.

1. Describe three qualities a hero must have. _____

_____

_____

_____

_____

2. Who is a hero to you? _____

3. Why do you feel this person is a hero? _____

_____

_____

_____

4. Do other people consider this person to be a hero? Explain. _____

_____

_____

_____

5. Does the world need heroes? Explain. _____

_____

_____

_____

_____

1.10 My Alter Ego

Directions: An *alter ego* is another side of a person that others do not often see. Answer the questions and write an article about your alter ego. Be sure to include an opening, body, and closing in your writing. Support your ideas with details and examples.

1. Describe how you believe others see you. (What kind of person do they

   consider you to be?) _____

   _____

   _____

   _____

2. Describe your alter ego. _____

   _____

   _____

3. When does your alter ego most often appear? _____

   _____

4. Why does your alter ego appear? _____

   _____

5. How do people react to your alter ego? _____

   _____

   _____

6. What is your opinion of your alter ego? Explain. _____

   _____

   _____

   _____

1.11 Responsibilities

Directions: Think of your responsibilities. Some of your responsibilities might include doing well in school, watching a younger brother or sister, or helping your parents with the chores around the house. Answer the questions and write an article about your responsibilities. Be sure to include an opening, body, and closing in your writing. Support your ideas with details and examples.

1. What are some of your responsibilities? _____

   _____

   _____

   _____

   _____

2. Give some examples of how you handle these responsibilities. _____

   _____

   _____

   _____

3. Why are these responsibilities important? _____

   _____

   _____

   _____

   _____

4. How do you feel about your responsibilities? _____

   _____

   _____

   _____

Personally Speaking

1.12 Big Thrill

Directions: Think of a time you took part in or watched an exciting event. Answer the questions and write a narrative about this experience. Be sure to include an opening, body, and closing in your writing. Support your ideas with details and examples.

1. What was the event? _____

2. When and where did it take place? _____

3. Who was with you? _____

_____

4. Describe what happened. _____

_____

_____

_____

_____

_____

5. Why was the event thrilling? _____

_____

_____

_____

6. What was the best part of this thrilling event? Explain. _____

_____

_____

_____

_____

1.13 Admiration

Directions: Think about someone you admire. This person might be living, or might have lived in the past. Answer the questions and write an article about this person. Be sure to include an opening, body, and closing in your writing. Support your ideas with details and examples.

1. Who is the person you admire? _____

2. Describe this person. _____

   _____

   _____

   _____

   _____

   _____

   _____

3. Why do you admire this person? _____

   _____

   _____

   _____

   _____

   _____

4. How has this person influenced your life? Explain. _____

   _____

   _____

   _____

   _____

   _____

1.14 Talent

> **Directions:** Everyone has special talents. Think about what you do better than other people. Answer the questions and write about your special talent. Be sure to include an opening, body, and closing in your writing. Support your ideas with details and examples.

1. What is your special talent? _____

_____

2. What skills, knowledge, or ability does this talent require? _____

_____

_____

_____

3. How did you acquire or develop this talent? _____

_____

_____

_____

4. What advice could you give others so that they may develop this talent?

_____

_____

_____

5. How might you improve your special talent? _____

_____

_____

_____

_____

1.15 The Most Meaningful Thing in My Life

Directions: Think about something that holds great meaning for you. Answer the questions and write an article about this meaningful thing in your life. Be sure to use an opening, body, and closing in your writing. Support your ideas with details and examples.

1. What is most meaningful to you? _____

_____

2. Why is this meaningful? _____

_____

_____

_____

_____

_____

3. What do you do to show that this is important to you? _____

_____

_____

_____

_____

_____

4. How would your life be different if this were not a part of your life?

_____

_____

_____

_____

_____

_____

1.16 Friends

Directions: Think about your friends. What makes a person a friend? Answer the questions and write an article explaining what you believe a friend is. Be sure to include an opening, body, and closing in your writing. Support your ideas with details and examples.

1. Describe what you believe a friend is. _____

_____

_____

_____

2. Name three traits every friend should have and give an example of each.

_____

_____

_____

_____

_____

_____

_____

_____

_____

3. Why are friends important? _____

_____

_____

_____

_____

_____

1.17 Advice for Getting Along

Directions: Think about people you know who get along well with others. Now think about some people who do not get along with others. Answer the questions, then write an article offering advice about how people can get along with others. Be sure to include an opening, body, and closing in your writing. Support your ideas with details and examples.

1. Why is it necessary that people get along? _____

   _____

   _____

   _____

2. What is one thing people should do if they hope to get along with others? Provide an example. _____

   _____

   _____

   _____

3. What is another thing people should do if they hope to get along with others? Provide an example. _____

   _____

   _____

   _____

4. What is a third thing people should do if they hope to get along with others? Provide an example. _____

   _____

   _____

   _____

Friends

1.18 Great Times with Friends

Friends

Directions: Think of a great time you had with a friend or friends. Maybe you went to a party, a sports event, or an amusement park. Or maybe you were just hanging out. Answer the questions, then write a narrative about an enjoyable time you had together. Be sure to include an opening, body, and closing in your writing. Support your ideas with details and examples.

1. Who is your friend, or friends? _____

2. Where did you go? _____

3. When did you go? _____

4. Who else was present? _____

_____

5. Describe this great time. What did you do? What happened? _____

_____

_____

_____

_____

_____

6. What was the best part of this great time? _____

_____

7. Why was this time so great? _____

_____

_____

_____

1.19 Adventure Among Friends

Directions: Think about a time when you shared an adventure with a friend or friends. Answer the questions and write a narrative about your adventure. Be sure to include an opening, body, and closing in your writing. Support your ideas with details and examples.

1. Where did this adventure take place? _____

2. When did this adventure take place? _____

3. Who was with you? _____

4. Describe the setting of this adventure. _____

_____

_____

5. Describe what happened. _____

_____

_____

_____

_____

_____

_____

6. How did the adventure end? _____

_____

_____

_____

_____

Friends

1.20 When You Need a Friend

Directions: Good friends are always willing to help each other. Think of a time you helped a friend, or a friend helped you. Answer the questions and write a narrative about this experience. Be sure to include an opening, body, and closing in your writing. Support your ideas with details and examples.

1. Who is your friend? _____

2. How long have you been friends? _____

3. When did you help your friend? (Or when did your friend help you?)
_____

4. Why did your friend (or you) need help? _____
_____
_____

5. How was the help given? _____
_____
_____
_____
_____

6. What happened after the help was given? _____
_____
_____
_____

Friends

1.21 Book Tip for a Friend

1. What book would you like your friend to read? _____

2. Who is the author? _____

3. Describe the main characters in the book. _____

_____

_____

_____

4. What is the setting of the story? _____

5. Describe the book's plot (but do not reveal the ending). _____

_____

_____

6. What is the theme, or message, of the book? _____

_____

7. Why did you like this book? _____

_____

_____

8. Why do you think your friend would like this book? _____

_____

_____

Friends

1.22 Friendly Character

Directions: Think of some favorite characters in some of your favorite stories or novels. Which of these characters would you most like to have as a friend? Answer the questions, then write an article explaining why this character would make a good friend. Be sure to include an opening, body, and closing in your writing. Support your ideas with details and examples.

1. What is the name of the character you would like to have as a friend?

   _____

2. What is the title of the story where you first "met" this character?

   _____

3. Describe the character. _____

   _____

   _____

   _____

4. Describe the story. (Be sure to mention the setting and plot.) _____

   _____

   _____

   _____

   _____

5. Explain what traits this character has that would

   make him or her a good friend. _____

   _____

   _____

   _____

1.23 Biographical Sketch of a Friend

Directions: A *biography* is a true story of a person's life that is written by another person. A *biographical sketch* is a short biography. Answer the questions and write a biographical sketch of a friend. Be sure to include an opening, body, and closing in your biography. Support your ideas with details and examples.

1. What is the name of your friend? _____

2. When and where was your friend born? _____

3. Describe your friend. _____

_____

_____

4. Describe your friend's family. _____

_____

_____

5. Does your friend have any pets? If so, describe them. _____

_____

6. Describe some things your friend likes. _____

_____

_____

7. Describe some things your friend dislikes. _____

_____

_____

8. What are your friend's plans for the future? _____

_____

_____

_____

Friends

1.24 Trouble

Directions: Imagine that a friend tells you that he or she is in terrible trouble. What would you do? Answer the questions and write a story about how you help your friend. Be sure to include interesting characters, a descriptive setting, an exciting plot, and a climax to your story.

1. What is your friend's name? _____

2. Describe your friend. _____
   _____
   _____

3. Name and describe any other main characters in the story. _____
   _____
   _____

4. Describe the setting of the story. _____
   _____

5. What trouble is your friend in? _____
   _____
   _____

6. How do you help your friend get out of trouble? _____
   _____
   _____

7. Describe the climax of your story. _____
   _____
   _____
   _____

Friends

1.25 Friends in Opposition

Directions: Imagine that two friends argue. What might happen? How might they feel? Answer the questions and write a story about two friends who have an argument. Be sure to include interesting characters, a descriptive setting, an exciting plot, and a climax to your story.

1. What are the names of the main characters in your story? _____
_____

2. Describe each of the main characters. _____
_____
_____

3. Describe the setting of the story. _____
_____

4. When did the argument occur? _____
_____

5. What caused the argument? _____
_____
_____

6. Describe the argument. _____
_____

7. How was the argument resolved? _____
_____
_____

Friends

1.26 What You Need to Know About My School

Directions: Schools around the country are a lot alike. But each is a little different, too. Think about your school. What is it like? Answer the questions and write an article describing your school. Be sure to use an opening, body, and closing in your writing. Support your ideas with details and examples.

1. What is the name of your school? _____

2. In what town and state is your school? _____

3. What grades and about how many students attend your school?

_____

4. Describe your school (classrooms, gym, cafeteria, computer room,

auditorium, and so on). _____

_____

_____

_____

5. Describe the subjects you learn in school. _____

_____

_____

6. Describe the extra activities your school offers (sports, music, and special

clubs). _____

_____

_____

7. Describe a typical school day. _____

_____

_____

School

1.27 Improving My School

Directions: An article in which an author writes about a problem or issue and encourages readers to support his or her ideas is an example of *persuasive writing*. Think about the good things in your school. Now think about things that can be improved. Answer the questions and write a persuasive article about how your school can be improved. Be sure to include an opening, body, and closing in your writing. Support your ideas with details and examples.

1. Describe your school (size, number of students, grades, and so on).

   _____

   _____

   _____

2. Describe at least one thing in your school that you feel should be improved. Why should this be improved? _____

   _____

   _____

   _____

   _____

   _____

3. What could students do to help improve this? _____

   _____

4. What could teachers do to help improve this? _____

   _____

5. What could parents do to help improve this? _____

   _____

School

1.28 School Uniforms: Pro and Con

Directions: Many schools have a dress code. Some schools even require that students wear uniforms. Think about your feelings about wearing a uniform to school. Answer the questions and write an article about your feelings. Be sure to include an opening, body, and closing in your writing. Support your ideas with details and examples.

1. If your school requires students to wear uniforms, describe the uniforms.

_____

_____

_____

2. What are some benefits of wearing uniforms to school? _____

_____

_____

_____

_____

3. Why might students dislike wearing uniforms to school? _____

_____

_____

_____

_____

4. What is your opinion about school uniforms? Explain. _____

_____

_____

_____

_____

School

1.29 Student of the Month

Directions: Imagine that you are in charge of giving an award for the student of the month in your school. This award may be for excellence in a certain subject, or it may be for excellence in all subjects. It might be given to someone who does something special for the school. Answer the questions and write an article explaining your guidelines for this award. Be sure to include an opening, body, and closing for your article. Support your ideas with details and examples.

1. What is the name of your award? _____

2. What is the award for? _____

_____

3. What are the criteria for winning this award? (What will a student have to

   do to earn this award?) _____

_____

_____

_____

_____

_____

4. What will the award be? _____

_____

5. Who will decide if a student has met the criteria for earning this award?

   Why is this person (or these persons) a good choice to make this decision?

_____

_____

_____

_____

School

1.30 Lunchroom Food

Directions: School food is, well, school food. Most students eat it, but few like it. Imagine that you can choose the food your school will serve for lunch. Answer the questions and write an article about your choices for school lunches. (Try to choose healthy foods.) Be sure to include an opening, body, and closing in your writing. Support your ideas with details and examples.

1. What kinds of food does your school serve for lunch? _____
_____
_____

2. What is your opinion of these foods? _____
_____
_____

3. What foods would you like your school to serve for the main part of lunch? Why? _____
_____
_____
_____

4. What foods would you like for dessert? Why? _____
_____

5. What types of beverages would you like served with lunch? Why?
_____

6. If your school has snack machines that students can use, what types of snacks should be offered? Why? _____
_____
_____

School

1.31 No (or Yes) to Homework

Directions: Although few students like homework, most receive homework at least a few times each week. Think about how much homework you receive. Answer the questions and write a personal opinion piece explaining your feelings about homework. Remember to include an opening, body, and closing in your writing. Support your ideas with details and examples.

1. Why is homework important? _____

_____

_____

2. When might homework not be important? Explain. _____

_____

_____

3. How much homework do you feel should be given each night? Explain.

_____

_____

4. Do you feel homework should be given on the weekends? Holidays?

Explain. _____

_____

_____

_____

5. Would it help or hurt students if they never got any homework? Explain.

_____

_____

_____

School

1.32 My Top Picks for Subjects

Directions: Think of all the subjects you are studying in school this year. Which are your favorites? Answer the questions and write an article about your favorite subjects. Be sure to include an opening, body, and closing in your writing. Support your ideas with details and examples.

1. What subjects are you studying this year? _____

_____

2. Which are your favorites? _____

3. Why are these your favorites? _____

_____

_____

_____

_____

_____

4. How might learning these subjects now help you in the future?

_____

_____

_____

_____

5. Do you ever use what you learn in these subjects outside of school?

Explain. _____

_____

_____

_____

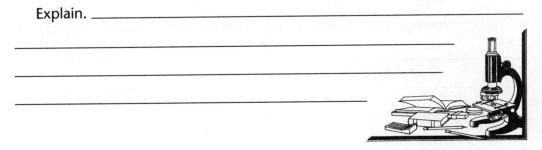

School

1.33 Honor Rolls

Directions: The purpose of an honor roll is to recognize students who attain high grades. But some schools do not have honor rolls. People in these schools believe honor rolls are not needed. Does your school have an honor roll? If so, should it be continued? If not, should one be started? Answer the questions and write an opinion piece sharing your feelings about an honor roll in your school. Remember to include an opening, body, and closing in your writing. Support your ideas with details and examples.

1. List reasons why a school should have an honor roll. _____

_____

_____

_____

2. List reasons why a school should not have an honor roll. _____

_____

_____

_____

3. To whom is an honor roll more important—students, teachers, or parents? Explain. _____

_____

_____

_____

4. Should your school have an honor roll? Explain. _____

_____

_____

_____

School

1.34 Physical Description of My Classroom

Directions: Look around your classroom. Notice how things are arranged. Answer the questions and write a description of your classroom. Remember to include an opening, body, and closing in your writing. Be sure to include good details.

1. Start at one corner and look around your classroom. List some of the objects you see. _____

   _____

   _____

   _____

2. Write details of these objects (for example, size, shape, and color).

   _____

   _____

   _____

   _____

   _____

   _____

3. Describe the furniture and how it is arranged. _____

   _____

4. Describe any tables and study stations. _____

   _____

5. Describe any special items (aquarium, plants, computers, and so on) in your classroom. _____

   _____

   _____

School

1.35 Special Event

Directions: Your school probably has special events throughout the year such as book fairs, science exhibits, and assemblies. For this writing assignment, take notes during a special event at your school. Answer the questions, then write a review of this event. Be sure to include an opening, body, and closing in your writing. Support your ideas with details and examples.

1. What was this event? _____

2. When and where did the event take place? _____

3. Who attended the event? _____

4. Describe the event. _____

   _____

   _____

   _____

   _____

5. Describe at least one thing you liked about the event. Why did you like

   this? _____

   _____

   _____

6. Describe at least one thing you did not like about the event. Why did you

   not like this? _____

   _____

   _____

7. What was your opinion of the event? Explain. _____

   _____

   _____

School

1.36 School Greatness

Directions: Most students like some things about their schools. They might feel their school has the best kids, the best drama club, or the best band. Think about what you feel is best about your school. Answer the questions and write an article about something great in your school. Be sure to include an opening, body, and closing in your writing. Support your ideas with details and examples.

1. What do you feel is great about your school? _____
   _____

2. Explain why you feel this is great. _____
   _____
   _____
   _____

3. How has your school achieved this greatness? (Include the efforts of
   students, teachers, and parents.) _____
   _____
   _____
   _____
   _____

4. What does this greatness mean for students? _____
   _____
   _____
   _____
   _____

School

1.37 School Rules

School

> **Directions:** Imagine that you could set up your school's rules. What rules would you make? Answer the questions and write about your rules. Remember to include an opening, body, and closing in your writing. Support your ideas with details and examples.

1. Write at least three rules you would make to help your school run smoothly. _____

   _____

   _____

2. How would these rules help your school run smoothly? _____

   _____

   _____

   _____

3. Do you think most students would agree that your rules are helpful? Explain. _____

   _____

   _____

   _____

4. What consequences would there be for breaking your rules? Explain.

   _____

   _____

   _____

   _____

1.38 New Student

Directions: Imagine that your teacher has chosen you to show a new student around your school. Answer the questions and write a story about this. Include interesting characters, a descriptive setting, an exciting plot, and a climax in your story.

1. Describe the characters in your story. _____

_____

_____

2. How might a new student feel in a new school? Give some examples.

_____

_____

3. To whom would you introduce this new student? Why? _____

_____

_____

4. What places in your school would you show the new student? Why?

_____

_____

5. What (if anything) would you warn the new student about? _____

_____

_____

6. Will the new student like your school? Explain. _____

_____

_____

_____

School

1.39 Perfect School

Directions: Imagine that you have the power to create a perfect school. This school could be everything you would want it to be. Answer the questions and write an article about your perfect school. Be sure to include an opening, body, and closing in your writing. Support your ideas with details and examples.

1. Where would the perfect school be located? Why? _____
_____

2. How long would the school day and the school year be? _____
_____

3. What grades would attend the school? About how many students would
   be in each class? _____

4. What subjects would students in this school study? Why would these
   subjects be required? _____
_____
_____

5. What special features would the school have? (For example, a big
   gymnasium, a swimming pool, tennis courts, computer lab?) _____
_____

6. What would be the most important rule in the school? Why would this be
   the most important? _____
_____

7. Would students receive a good education at this school? Explain.
_____
_____

School

140 Home Sweet Home

Directions: Think about where you live and what makes your home special. Answer the questions and write a description of your home. Remember to include an opening, body, and closing in your writing. Support your ideas with details and examples.

1. Where do you live? _____

2. Describe your neighborhood or the area around your home. _____

   _____

   _____

3. Describe the climate where you live. _____

   _____

   _____

4. Describe your home. _____

   _____

   _____

   _____

5. What is special about your home? _____

   _____

   _____

6. Do you like living here? Why or why not? _____

   _____

   _____

   _____

   _____

1.41 Round About

1. Describe three places in your city or town (or in the area nearby) that visitors might be interested in seeing. _____

   _____

   _____

   _____

   _____

   _____

2. What do you think visitors would like best about your city or town? Why?

   _____

   _____

   _____

   _____

3. What do you think visitors would like least about your city or town? Why?

   _____

   _____

   _____

   _____

   _____

Out and About

1.42 Customs and Traditions

Directions: Most cities and towns have special customs and traditions. They might have a Founder's Day, a Memorial Day parade, or a fireworks display on the Fourth of July. Think about some of the customs or traditions in the city or town where you live. Answer the questions and write an article about one of them. Be sure to include an opening, body, and closing in your writing. Support your ideas with details and examples.

1. What is a custom or tradition of your city or town? _____

_____

2. How often is this custom or tradition celebrated? _____

3. Where is it celebrated? _____

4. When is it celebrated? _____

5. Who takes an active part in the celebration? _____

_____

_____

6. What, if any, special preparations are made before the celebration?

_____

7. Describe this custom or tradition and its celebration. _____

_____

_____

8. What is your favorite part of this custom or tradition? Explain. _____

_____

_____

1.43 Improvements Needed

Directions: Think about how your city or town could be improved. Maybe more parks could be opened. Maybe there could be more activities for kids. Or maybe a public swimming pool could be built. Answer the questions and write an article about how your city or town could be improved. Remember to include an opening, body, and closing in your writing. Support your ideas with details and examples.

1. What is the name of your city or town, and where is it located?

_____

2. Describe your city or town. _____

_____

_____

_____

_____

3. Name at least one thing that can be improved. _____

_____

4. Why should this be improved? _____

_____

_____

_____

5. How might it be improved? _____

_____

_____

_____

_____

Out and About

1.44 Hanging Out

Directions: Think about a place where you and your friends hang out to have fun, relax, or just pass time. Maybe this place is a recreation center, a park, or someone's house. Answer the questions and write an article describing this place. Remember to include an opening, body, and closing in your writing. Support your ideas with details and examples.

1. Where do you and your friends hang out? _____

2. Describe this place. _____

_____

_____

_____

3. With whom do you usually hang out at this place? _____

_____

4. What do you do there? _____

_____

_____

_____

_____

_____

5. Explain why you hang out there. _____

_____

_____

_____

_____

Out and About

1.45 State of Affairs

Directions: Every state has many interesting places to visit. Think of your state and an interesting place you visited. Answer the questions and write an article about this place. Remember to include an opening, body, and closing in your writing. Support your ideas with details and examples.

1. What is this place? _____

2. Where is this place located? _____

3. When did you visit this place? _____

4. With whom did you go? _____

5. Describe this place. _____

_____

_____

_____

_____

6. Why did you find it interesting? _____

_____

_____

_____

7. Do you think others would find it interesting? Explain. _____

_____

_____

8. Would you like to visit this place again? Explain. _____

_____

_____

Out and About

1.46 My Special Place

Directions: Most people have a special place they go when they need to be alone, relax, or get "unstressed." This place might be their room, the back porch, or even a treehouse. Answer the questions and write an article about your special place. Be sure to include an opening, body, and closing in your writing. Support your ideas with details and examples.

1. Where is your special place? _____

2. Describe this place. _____

_____

_____

_____

_____

3. When do you go to this place? _____

_____

_____

4. Why do you go there? _____

_____

_____

_____

5. How does this place make you feel? Explain. _____

_____

_____

_____

_____

1.47 Incredible Vacation

Directions: Vacations can be times of great fun. Think of a vacation that you had. It might have been with your parents, relatives, or friends. Answer the questions and write a narrative about this vacation. Be sure to include an opening, body, and closing in your writing. Support your ideas with details and examples.

1. Where did you go for this vacation? _____

2. When did you go? _____

3. With whom did you go? _____

4. How did you travel to your destination? _____

5. How long was your vacation? _____

6. Describe where you stayed. _____

_____

_____

7. Describe the highlights of your vacation. _____

_____

_____

_____

_____

8. What was better about this vacation than any other you have taken?

   Explain. _____

_____

_____

_____

Out and About

1.48 Travel Firsts

Directions: Think back to a travel first—the first time you traveled in a train, sailed on a ship, flew in a plane, or maybe rode a horse. Answer the questions and write a narrative about this travel first. Be sure to include an opening, body, and closing in your writing. Support your ideas with details and examples.

1. What was your travel first? _____

2. When did you first travel in this way, and how old were you? _____
_____

3. Where did you go? _____

4. Who was with you? _____

5. Describe your feelings about this travel first. _____
_____
_____
_____

6. Describe the trip. _____
_____
_____
_____

7. Have you ever traveled like this again? If so, explain how the other times
   were different from the first. _____
_____
_____
_____

1.49 Travel Advice

Directions: Imagine that a friend plans to go on vacation to a place that you have already visited. This might be a big amusement park, a cottage at a lake, or a trip to the city. Your friend asks you about this place and what to expect. Answer the questions, then write a letter of travel advice to your friend. Support your ideas with details and examples.

1. What is your friend's destination? _____

2. Where would you suggest that your friend stay? Why? _____

_____

_____

3. What activities and attractions will your friend find there? _____

_____

4. Which ones would you recommend that your friend try? Why?

_____

_____

5. Describe the kind of weather your friend should expect. _____

_____

6. What kinds of clothing should your friend bring? _____

_____

7. What types of equipment should your friend bring? (For example, swimsuit, fishing poles, skis, sunglasses, sunscreen.) _____

_____

8. What would you caution your friend about? Explain. _____

_____

_____

Out and About

1.50 Travel Calamities

Directions: Have you ever had something go wrong when you were traveling? The car might have broken down. Bad weather might have made your family miss their flight. Or you might have gone sailing and gotten seasick. Imagine going somewhere and everything goes wrong. Answer the questions and write a story about travel calamities. Create interesting characters, a descriptive setting, an exciting plot, and a climax for your story.

1. Name and describe the main characters in your story. _____

_____

_____

_____

2. Where are the characters going? _____

3. Why are they going there? _____

4. How are they traveling? _____

5. Describe things that go wrong. _____

_____

_____

_____

6. How do the characters solve the calamities they face? _____

_____

_____

_____

7. Do they reach their destination on time? Explain. _____

_____

Out and About

1.51 Vacation Mystery

Directions: A *mystery* is a story in which the characters try to solve a crime or figure out a puzzling problem. Mysteries can be as much fun to write as they are to read. Imagine going on vacation only to become involved in a mystery. Answer the questions and write a story about the mystery you must solve. Be sure to create interesting characters, a descriptive setting, an exciting plot, and a climax for your story.

1. Where and when does this story take place? _____

_____

2. Along with yourself, name and describe the main characters in your story.

_____

_____

_____

_____

3. Describe the setting of the story. _____

_____

4. Describe the mystery. _____

_____

_____

5. Describe some clues that help you solve the mystery. _____

_____

_____

6. How do you solve the mystery? _____

_____

_____

Out and About

1.52 Lost

Directions: Imagine that you or a friend has lost something of value. Answer the questions and write a story about finding what was lost. Be sure to create interesting characters, a descriptive setting, an exciting plot, and a climax for your story.

1. Where and when does this story take place? _____
   _____

2. Name and describe the main characters. _____
   _____
   _____
   _____

3. Describe the setting. _____
   _____

4. Describe what was lost. _____
   _____

5. How did this become lost? _____
   _____
   _____

6. How do the characters try to find what was lost? _____
   _____
   _____

7. How do they finally find what was lost? (Or are they unsuccessful?)
   _____
   _____

1.53 Strange Happenings

Directions: Imagine that strange things begin happening around your home, in your town, or in your neighborhood. Answer the questions and write a story about these occurrences. Be sure to create interesting characters, a descriptive setting, an exciting plot, and a climax for your story.

1. Where and when does the story take place? _____

   _____

2. Name and describe the main characters. _____

   _____

   _____

3. Describe the setting. _____

   _____

4. What strange things occur? _____

   _____

   _____

5. What do you do to discover the cause of the strange occurrences?

   _____

   _____

6. What do you find the cause to be? _____

   _____

7. Describe the climax of the story. _____

   _____

   _____

Out and About

1.54 Tunes

Directions: Think of your favorite kind of music. Answer the questions, then write an article about the music you enjoy the most. Remember to include an opening, body, and closing in your writing. Support your ideas with details and examples.

1. What kind of music do you most like to listen to? _____

2. Describe this kind of music. _____

_____

_____

_____

3. What makes this music different from other kinds of music? _____

_____

_____

_____

4. Is this music popular? Explain. _____

_____

_____

5. Which singer or group that performs this music is your favorite? Why?

_____

_____

6. Why do you like this type of music? Explain. _____

_____

_____

_____

_____

At Your Leisure

1.55 Star Singers

1. Who is your favorite singer or musical group? _____

_____

2. Is this singer or group popular throughout the country? Explain.

_____

_____

3. What type of music does this singer or group perform? _____

_____

4. What do you feel is the best song of this singer or group? Why do you feel

this song is the best? _____

_____

_____

5. How is this singer or group different from others? _____

_____

_____

_____

6. Why is this singer or group your favorite? Explain. _____

_____

_____

_____

At Your Leisure

1.56 What the Song Says to Me

Directions: Most songwriters try to share ideas through their songs. The message they wish to share with their listeners is in the *lyrics* (words) of the song. Choose a favorite song and think about the message of the songwriter. Answer the questions and write an article about what the song means to you. Be sure to include an opening, body, and closing in your writing. Support your ideas with details and examples.

1. What is the title of your favorite song? _____

2. Who wrote and recorded the song? _____

3. What is the song about? _____

_____

_____

4. What do you like best about the song? Lyrics? Music? Something else? Explain. _____

_____

_____

5. Which lyrics do you like the best? Why? _____

_____

_____

6. What is the message the songwriter is trying to share? Explain.

_____

_____

7. Why do you like this song? Explain. _____

_____

_____

At Your Leisure

1.57 Book Review

Directions: A *book review* tells a reader what a book is about. It should include the reviewer's opinion of the book. Think about a book you recently read. Answer the questions and write a review of this book. Be sure to include an opening, body, and closing in your review. Support your ideas with details and examples.

1. What is the title of your book? _____

2. Who is the author? _____

3. Who is the publisher and when was the book published? _____

4. What type of book, or genre, is it? (Is it nonfiction or fiction? If fiction, is it fantasy, adventure, history?) _____

5. Explain what the book is about. (For fiction, describe the setting, characters, and plot, but do not tell the ending.) _____

_____

_____

_____

_____

_____

6. If your book is fiction, what is its theme? _____

_____

7. Did you like this book? Explain. _____

_____

_____

_____

At Your Leisure

1.58 Video Game Review

Directions: Writing a review of a video game can be a lot of fun. You have to play the game before you can write about it. Think of a video game you enjoy. Answer the questions and write a review of this game. Remember to include an opening, body, and closing in your review. Support your ideas with details and examples.

1. What is the name of this video game? _____

2. For which age levels is it recommended? Is this game suitable for these

   ages? Explain. _____

   _____

3. Describe the action of the game. _____

   _____

   _____

   _____

   _____

4. What must a player do to win? _____

   _____

5. What strategies can you suggest that will help a player to win?

   _____

   _____

   _____

6. What type of person will probably like this game? Why? _____

   _____

   _____

1.59 Favorites

Directions: Think of something you enjoy doing. Maybe you enjoy sports, or reading, or hobbies. Answer the questions and write an article about your favorite thing to do. Be sure to include an opening, body, and closing in your writing. Support your ideas with details and examples.

1. What is your favorite thing to do? _____

2. When, where, and with whom (if anyone) do you enjoy this? _____

   _____

   _____

3. Who introduced you to this activity? _____

4. Describe your favorite thing to do. _____

   _____

   _____

   _____

   _____

   _____

   _____

   _____

   _____

5. Why is this your favorite thing to do? Explain. _____

   _____

   _____

   _____

   _____

   _____

At Your Leisure

1.60 Special Day

Directions: Imagine you could spend a day doing anything you wished. What would you do? Answer the questions and write an article about this special day. Remember to include an opening, body, and closing in your writing. Support your ideas with details and examples.

1. Where would you go on this special day? _____
_____

2. With whom (if anyone) would you spend this day? Why? _____
_____
_____

3. Describe all you would do on this special day. _____
_____
_____
_____
_____
_____
_____
_____

4. Why would this day be so special? Explain. _____
_____
_____
_____
_____
_____

At Your Leisure

1.61 Movie Review

Directions: Think of a movie you watched recently. Answer the questions and write a review of this movie. Be sure to include an opening, body, and closing in your review. Support your ideas with details and examples.

1. What is the name of the movie? _____

2. Describe the main characters. _____

    _____

    _____

3. Describe the setting of the movie. _____

    _____

4. Describe the quality of the acting. _____

    _____

5. Summarize the plot of the movie. _____

    _____

    _____

    _____

    _____

6. Describe the best scene. _____

    _____

    _____

7. Would you recommend this movie to your friends? Explain. _____

    _____

At Your Leisure

1.62 TV Time

Directions: Think about how much TV you watch each day. Answer the questions, then write an article about your TV viewing habits. Remember to include an opening, body, and closing in your writing. Support your ideas with details and examples.

1. About how much TV do you watch each day? _____

2. Do you think the amount of TV you watch is too much, just about right, or too little? Explain. _____
_____

3. What types of TV shows do you enjoy the most? Why? _____
_____
_____
_____

4. What types of TV shows do you enjoy the least? Why? _____
_____
_____
_____

5. How might you benefit from watching TV? Explain. _____
_____
_____

6. How might TV watching be detrimental, or harmful, to you? Explain.
_____
_____
_____

At Your Leisure

1.63 Changing Character

Directions: In most stories, the main characters change during the story. They may learn something new about themselves, or they may learn something new about life. Think of one of your favorite characters in a story you read. Answer the questions and write an article about how the character changed. Be sure to include an opening, body, and closing in your writing. Support your ideas with details and examples.

1. What is the title of the story? _____

2. What is the name of this character? _____

3. Describe the story. (Include characters, setting, and plot.) _____

_____

_____

_____

_____

4. Describe this character at the beginning of the story and at the end.

_____

_____

5. Describe the changes in this character. _____

_____

6. What caused these changes? Explain. _____

_____

7. At the end of the story, was the character a better person? Why or why not?

   not? _____

_____

_____

At Your Leisure

1.64 Lunchtime Fantasy

Directions: Imagine having lunch with a celebrity or otherwise famous person of your choice. Answer the questions and write about this fantasy lunch. Be sure to include an opening, body, and closing in your writing. Support your ideas with details and examples.

1. With whom would you have lunch? _____

2. Why would you choose this person? _____
   _____
   _____

3. Where would you have lunch? _____

4. What would you have for lunch? _____
   _____

5. If you could ask this person three questions, what would they be? Why would you ask these questions? _____
   _____
   _____
   _____

6. What do you think the answers would be? _____
   _____
   _____
   _____
   _____

At Your Leisure

1.65 Great Gizmo

Directions: Think of a product you are very pleased with—for example, a new computer system, a pair of in-line skates, or a DVD player for your room. Answer the questions and write an article describing this product to others. Remember to include an opening, body, and closing in your writing. Support your ideas with details and examples.

1. What is the product? _____

2. Where can people purchase this product? _____

3. Describe the product and what it does. _____

_____

_____

_____

_____

4. How do you benefit from this product? Why are you so satisfied with it?

_____

_____

_____

_____

5. What, if anything, could make this product even better? Explain.

_____

_____

_____

_____

_____

At Your Leisure

1.66 Changing Places

Directions: Imagine that you and a lead character of one of your favorite stories changed places. You are now the character in the story, and you change the ending. Answer the questions and write a new ending to the story. Create interesting characters, a descriptive setting, an exciting plot, and a climax for the new ending of the story.

1. What is the title of the story you are in? _____

2. Which character did you replace? _____

3. Why did you choose to replace this character? _____

_____

_____

4. Describe the original story. (Include characters, setting, plot, and climax.)

_____

_____

_____

_____

_____

_____

_____

5. Describe the new climax. _____

_____

_____

_____

At Your Leisure

1.67 Funhouse of Fear

Directions: Imagine going in a funhouse that had no way out. Answer the questions and write a story about how you escaped this terrifying funhouse. Create interesting characters, a descriptive setting, an exciting plot, and a climax for your story.

1. Where is the funhouse located? _____

2. Name and describe the main characters in your story. _____

   _____

   _____

3. Describe the setting. _____

   _____

4. Describe the funhouse. _____

   _____

   _____

   _____

5. Why were you unable to find your way out? _____

   _____

   _____

   _____

6. How did you finally escape the funhouse? _____

   _____

   _____

   _____

At Your Leisure

1.68 Games People Play

Directions: Think of a game you like to play. It might be a computer game, a board game, or a card game. Answer the questions and write an article about this game. Be sure to include an opening, body, and closing in your writing. Support your ideas with details and examples.

1. What is the name of this game? _____

2. When did you learn to play this game? _____

3. Who taught you how to play? _____

4. When do you play this game? _____

5. Does the game require teams? Explain. _____

_____

_____

6. Describe the game. (Include the object of the game and its basic rules.)

_____

_____

_____

_____

7. What strategies or techniques can help someone win? _____

_____

_____

8. Why do you enjoy this game? Explain. _____

_____

_____

Name _____ Date _____

1.69 Great Sport

Directions: Think about the sports you enjoy. Answer the questions and write an article about your favorite sport. Remember to include an opening, body, and closing in your writing. Support your ideas with details and examples.

1. What is your favorite sport? _____

2. Which do you enjoy more—playing or watching this sport? Explain.

   _____

   _____

3. If teams are necessary for this sport, how many players are on a team?

   _____

4. Explain what, if any, special positions the team has. _____

   _____

5. Describe the field, court, or playing surface on which this sport is played.

   _____

6. What equipment, if any, is necessary to compete in this sport? _____

   _____

7. Does this sport include a game? If yes, describe the object of the game

   and how the game is played. (If the sport does not include a game, explain

   how a person participates in the sport.) _____

   _____

   _____

8. Why do you like this sport? _____

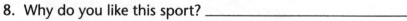

   _____

   _____

1.70 Superstar

Directions: Think of an athlete you admire. This athlete might be a star in a major sport like baseball, tennis, or soccer, or in an extreme sport like skateboarding, snowboarding, or motocross. Answer the questions and write an article about this superstar and his or her sport. Be sure to include an opening, body, and closing in your writing. Support your ideas with details and examples.

1. Who is the superstar athlete? _____

2. In which sport is this person a superstar? _____

3. If this athlete plays on a team, what is the team? What position does he or she play? _____

4. What are this athlete's greatest skills? What makes this person better than others at this sport? _____

_____

_____

_____

_____

5. What tournaments or championships, if any, has this athlete won?

_____

6. What records, if any, has he or she broken? _____

7. What makes this athlete a superstar? _____

_____

_____

_____

_____

1.71 One Fine Day

Directions: Imagine that you could have a day in which you could do whatever you wished. Everything would be perfect. Answer the questions and write about this fine day. Remember to include an opening, body, and closing in your writing. Support your ideas with details and examples.

1. Where would you go on this day? _____

2. Would anyone be with you? If yes, who? Why would you want this person, or people, to be with you? _____

_____

_____

3. Describe the place where you would be. _____

_____

_____

4. What would you do? _____

_____

_____

_____

_____

_____

5. What would make this day perfect? Explain. _____

_____

_____

_____

_____

Sports and Play

1.72 Rules for Spectators at Kids' Sports

Directions: Imagine that you could write the rules for how spectators should behave at kids' sporting events. Answer the questions and write an article explaining your rules for spectators. Be sure to include an opening, body, and closing in your writing. Support your ideas with details and examples.

1. How should spectators behave at kids' sporting events? _____
_____
_____

2. What are three rules for spectator behavior? _____
_____
_____
_____
_____
_____

3. Why are these rules important? _____
_____
_____
_____

4. What might happen if people do not practice courtesy and common sense when attending kids' sporting events? Explain. _____
_____
_____
_____
_____

1.73 Being the Best

Directions: Think of a time you were at your best. Maybe you were playing basketball. Maybe you were singing a solo in your school's spring concert. Maybe you were snowboarding down a huge hill. What-ever you were doing, you were at your very best. Answer the questions and write a narrative about this day. Remember to include an opening, body, and closing in your writing. Support your ideas with details and examples.

1. What were you doing when you were at your best? _____
   _____

2. When and where were you at your best? _____

3. Who was with you? _____

4. Describe how you were at your best. _____
   _____
   _____
   _____

5. Why do you think you were at your best? _____
   _____
   _____
   _____

6. Describe how you felt being your best. _____
   _____
   _____
   _____
   _____

1.74 Talent or Desire

Directions: Think about participating in sports, playing a musical instrument, dancing, cheerleading, or taking part in some other competitive activity. What is more important to being successful—talent or desire? Answer the questions and write an article about which is more important. Be sure to include an opening, body, and closing in your writing. Support your ideas with details and examples.

1. What must a person do to excel at sports, music, or other activities?

   _____

   _____

   _____

2. Is talent necessary to being successful? Explain. _____

   _____

   _____

   _____

3. Is desire necessary to being successful? Explain. _____

   _____

   _____

   _____

4. Which, talent or desire, is more important? Or are they equally important?

   Explain. _____

   _____

   _____

   _____

   _____

1.75 Exciting Event

Directions: Think of a time you were at an exciting event. For example, this might have been a baseball playoff game, a concert starring your favorite singer, or a monster truck show. Answer the questions and write about this event. Remember to include an opening, body, and closing in your writing. Support your ideas with details and examples.

1. What was this event? _____

2. Where and when did it take place? _____

3. Who was with you? _____

4. Describe the event. _____

_____

_____

_____

_____

_____

_____

_____

5. What made this event so exciting? Why? _____

_____

_____

_____

_____

_____

Sports and Play

1.76 New Game

Directions: Have you ever invented a game or created new rules for an old game? Answer the questions, then write an article about a new game or a new version of an old game you invented. Remember to include an opening, body, and closing in your writing. Support your ideas with details and examples.

1. What is the name of your new game? _____

2. When did you invent this game? _____

3. Who, if anyone, helped you invent the game? _____

4. What is the object of the game? _____

_____

5. Describe the game and its rules. _____

_____

_____

_____

_____

6. What strategies should a player use if the person hopes to win?

_____

_____

_____

7. Have others played your game? If yes, did they like it? Explain. _____

_____

_____

_____

1.77 Sportsmanship

> **Directions:** Think about sportsmanship and what it means. Answer the
> questions and write an article about being a good sport. Be sure to
> include an opening, body, and closing in your writing. Support your
> ideas with details and examples.

1. What is good sportsmanship? _____

   _____

   _____

2. Give some examples of good sportsmanship. _____

   _____

   _____

   _____

3. Is being a good sport important? Explain. _____

   _____

   _____

   _____

4. Do you agree or disagree with the following saying? "It's not whether you
   win or lose, it's how you play the game." Explain. _____

   _____

   _____

   _____

   _____

   _____

   _____

1.78 Consumer Review of a Sports Product

Directions: Think of sports equipment such as running shoes, a baseball glove, or a field hockey stick. Answer the questions, then write an article about a sports product, telling about its strengths and weaknesses. Be sure to include an opening, body, and closing in your writing. Support your ideas with details and examples.

1. What product are you reviewing? _____

2. Why are you qualified to review this product? (What experience do you have in using this product?) _____
_____

3. Describe the product. _____
_____
_____
_____

4. Describe its best features. _____
_____
_____

5. How might it be improved? _____
_____
_____

6. Would you recommend this product to others? Explain. _____
_____
_____
_____

1.79 Special Activity

Directions: Think of a special activity that you enjoy with family or friends. Maybe you visit amusement parks with your family. Maybe your family has a reunion each year. Or maybe you go to camp every summer with your friends. Answer the questions and write a narrative about your special activity. Remember to include an opening, body, and closing in your writing. Support your ideas with details and examples.

1. What is your special activity? _____

2. Who shares this activity with you? _____

3. Where and when do you enjoy this activity? _____
_____

4. Describe this activity. _____
_____
_____
_____
_____
_____
_____
_____

5. What makes this activity special? Explain. _____
_____
_____
_____
_____
_____

1.80 Competition

Directions: Think of a time you were in a great competition. Maybe you were in a dance competition. Maybe you were playing a challenging computer game. Maybe you were in a tennis tournament. Answer the questions and write a narrative about this competition. Be sure to include an opening, body, and closing in your writing. Support your ideas with details and examples.

1. What was the competition? _____

2. Against whom were you competing? _____

3. When and where was this competition? _____

_____

4. Describe the competition. (Especially note the toughest part.) _____

_____

_____

_____

_____

_____

5. What strategies or techniques did you use to try to win? _____

_____

_____

6. How did you win? Or why did you lose? Explain. _____

_____

_____

_____

1.81 Coach

Directions: Imagine that you are a coach. You might coach soccer, cheerleading, track, or some other activity. What advice could you give to students? Answer the questions and write an article about the advice you would give. Be sure to include an opening, body, and closing in your writing. Support your ideas with details and examples.

1. What sport or activity are you coaching? _____

2. What qualifications do you have to be a coach? (How much experience do you have with this sport or activity?) _____

   _____

   _____

   _____

3. What skills should students have if they want to do well in this sport or activity? _____

   _____

   _____

   _____

4. Is attitude important to being successful in this sport or activity? Explain.

   _____

   _____

5. What advice would you give to younger students who are just starting this sport or activity? _____

   _____

   _____

   _____

1.82 Big Game

> **Directions:** Imagine being a sports star and playing in the biggest game of your life. Answer the questions and write a story about this game. Create interesting characters, a descriptive setting, an exciting plot, and a climax for your story.

1. In what game are you playing? _____

2. Name and describe the main characters in the story. _____
   _____
   _____
   _____

3. Describe the setting. _____
   _____
   _____

4. Describe the plot of the story. _____
   _____
   _____
   _____
   _____
   _____
   _____

5. Describe the climax of the story. _____
   _____
   _____
   _____

1.83 UFOs (Unidentified Flying Objects)

Directions: Many people claim they have seen UFOs and extraterrestrials (beings from other planets). Answer the questions, then write an article sharing your thoughts about UFOs. Be sure to include an opening, body, and closing in your writing. Support your ideas with details and examples.

1. Have you or anyone you know ever seen a UFO? If yes, explain when and where. _____
_____

2. If you have seen a UFO, describe what you saw. _____
_____
_____

3. If you have not seen a UFO, do you believe they exist? Why or why not?
_____
_____
_____

4. Do you believe beings from other planets have visited Earth? Explain.
_____
_____
_____

5. Do you believe that life exists on other planets? Why or why not?
_____
_____
_____
_____

Weird, Strange, and Unbelievable

1.84 Inexplicable Occurrence

Directions: Everybody has seen or heard about strange occurrences that cannot be explained. Answer the questions, then write about an inexplicable occurrence you have seen or heard about. Remember to include an opening, body, and closing in your writing. Support your ideas with details and examples.

1. What was the occurrence? _____

2. Where and when did it happen? _____
_____

3. Who was with you? (Or how did you hear about it?) _____
_____

4. Describe what happened. _____
_____
_____
_____
_____
_____

5. How did you, or others, try to explain what happened? _____
_____
_____

6. Why did this event remain unexplained? _____
_____
_____

1.85 Chilling Nightmare

Directions: Everybody has nightmares. Some nightmares can be so frightening that we wake up in the night shaking and terrified. Answer the questions and write about your most terrifying nightmare. Be sure to include an opening, body, and closing in your writing. Support your ideas with details and examples.

1. What was your nightmare about? _____

_____

2. Who, or what, was in your nightmare? _____

3. Describe the setting of your nightmare. _____

_____

4. Describe what happened in your nightmare. _____

_____

_____

_____

5. Did you wake up during your nightmare? If yes, how did you feel?

_____

_____

6. Were you afraid to go back to sleep after waking up? Why or why not?

_____

_____

7. Why do you think you had this nightmare? _____

_____

_____

Weird, Strange, and Unbelievable

1.86 Making Magic

Directions: Imagine being given magic power that will allow you to cast only one spell. Answer the questions and write a story about your magic power and what you do with it. Create interesting characters, a descriptive setting, an exciting plot, and a climax for your story.

1. Describe the main characters in your story. _____
    _____
    _____
    _____

2. Describe the setting. _____
    _____

3. How did you receive your magic power? _____
    _____
    _____

4. What one act of magic did you perform? _____
    _____
    _____

5. Why did you perform this act? _____
    _____
    _____

6. What happened after you performed your magic? _____
    _____
    _____
    _____

1.87 Animal Diary

> **Directions:** Imagine if an animal that knows you could read and write. Now imagine if this animal kept a diary. Answer the questions and write a diary entry as if the entry was written by an animal acquaintance. Be sure to include great details in your writing.

1. What animal is the writer of the diary? _____

2. How does this animal know you? _____

3. Describe what this animal observes throughout the day. _____

_____

_____

4. Describe what it hears throughout the day. _____

_____

_____

5. Describe what it does most of the day. _____

_____

_____

6. What is the best part of this animal's day? _____

_____

7. What is the worst part of its day? _____

_____

8. Describe what this animal would say about you in the diary. _____

_____

_____

Weird, Strange, and Unbelievable

1.88 Historical Reporter

Directions: Imagine that you are a reporter living in the past. You are writing about an important event that happened. Answer the questions and write an article about this event. Be sure to include an opening, body, and closing in your writing. Support your ideas with details and examples.

1. What event are you writing about? _____

2. When and where did this event take place? _____

3. Who was involved in the event? _____
_____

4. Describe the event. _____
_____
_____
_____
_____
_____

5. Why did the event happen? _____
_____
_____
_____

6. What were the results of the event? _____
_____
_____
_____

Weird, Strange, and Unbelievable

1.89 Premonition

Directions: Imagine that you wake up one day with a premonition of a coming disaster. Answer the questions and write a story about how you try to prevent this disaster. Create interesting characters, a descriptive setting, an exciting plot, and a climax for your story.

1. Describe the main characters in your story. _____

_____

_____

2. Describe the setting. _____

_____

3. When did you first become aware of the premonition? _____

_____

4. Describe the premonition. _____

_____

5. How did you try to stop the disaster from happening? _____

_____

_____

_____

_____

_____

6. Were you successful? Why or why not? _____

_____

_____

_____

Weird, Strange, and Unbelievable

1.90 Extraterrestrial Students

Directions: Imagine that beings from another planet have come to Earth. These extraterrestrials are friendly and wish to learn about us. Some extraterrestrial students are visiting your school, and you have been asked to show them around. Answer the questions and write a story about the extraterrestrials in your school. Create interesting characters, a descriptive setting, a well-defined plot, and a climax for your story.

1. Describe the extraterrestrials who come to your school. _____

_____

2. Describe the human characters in your story. _____

_____

3. Describe the setting. _____

_____

4. Why were you chosen to show the extraterrestrials around? _____

_____

5. What did you show them? Why did you show them these things?

_____

_____

6. What did they find most interesting about your school? Why? _____

_____

_____

7. How did other students react to the extraterrestrials? Did their reactions cause tension? Explain. _____

_____

© Gary Robert Muschla

1.91 Cyberspace Hero

Directions: Think of your favorite video or online game. Imagine you are the star character of the game. Answer the questions and write a story about being a hero in cyberspace. Create interesting characters, a descriptive setting, an exciting plot, and a climax for your story.

1. What is the name of the game? _____

2. Describe the setting of the game. _____
   _____

3. Describe the main characters in the game. _____
   _____
   _____

4. Describe the object of the game. _____
   _____

5. Describe your attempts to win the game. What strategies did you use?
   _____
   _____
   _____

6. How did your enemies (or opponents) try to stop you? _____
   _____
   _____

7. Did you win the game? Explain. _____
   _____
   _____
   _____

Weird, Strange, and Unbelievable

1.92 The Spell

Directions: Imagine that an evil witch casts a spell on you. This spell forces you to say whatever you are thinking. Answer the questions and write a story about this terrible spell. Create interesting characters, a descriptive setting, an exciting plot, and a climax for your story.

1. Describe the main characters in your story. _____

_____

_____

2. Describe the setting. _____

_____

3. Why did the witch cast a spell on you? _____

_____

_____

4. Describe how the spell got you in trouble. _____

_____

_____

_____

_____

5. How did you manage to break the spell? _____

_____

_____

_____

_____

1.93 Carnival Coming to Town

Directions: Think about a carnival coming to your town or neighborhood. But this is not an ordinary carnival. Strange things happen, and the carnival poses a danger to you and your friends. Answer the questions and write a story about this carnival. Create interesting characters, a descriptive setting, an exciting plot, and a climax for your story.

1. Describe the main characters in this story. _____

_____

_____

2. Describe the setting. _____

_____

3. Describe the carnival. _____

_____

_____

_____

4. What danger did it pose? _____

_____

5. How did you overcome the danger? _____

_____

_____

_____

_____

_____

Weird, Strange, and Unbelievable

1.94 Big Switch

> **Directions:** Imagine that you could switch places with a plant or an animal for a day. You would become that plant or animal for twenty-four hours. Answer the questions and write a story about your experience. Create interesting characters, a descriptive setting, a well-defined plot, and a climax for your story.

1. With what plant or animal would you switch places? Why? _____
   _____
   _____

2. Where would you be after switching places? _____
   _____

3. Describe your "new" self. _____
   _____
   _____

4. What would you do? _____
   _____

5. Describe your senses. What you would see, hear, feel, smell, and taste?
   _____
   _____
   _____
   _____
   _____

6. What would be your greatest impression about switching places?

_____

1.95 The Shoes

Directions: Imagine if you were given a pair of running shoes that made you the fastest runner in the world. Answer the questions and write a story about these super shoes. Create interesting characters, a descriptive setting, an exciting plot, and a climax for your story.

1. Describe the main characters in your story. _____

_____

_____

2. Describe the setting. _____

_____

3. How did you obtain the shoes? _____

_____

_____

4. How did you discover their super speed? _____

_____

_____

5. What did you do after you learned about their speed? _____

_____

_____

_____

_____

6. Do you still have the running shoes? Explain. _____

_____

_____

Weird, Strange, and Unbelievable

1.96 Return to the Past

Directions: Imagine being able to go back to the past knowing everything you know now. Answer the questions and write a story about returning to the past. Create interesting characters, a descriptive setting, a well-defined plot, and a climax for your story.

1. Describe the main characters of your story. _____
   _____
   _____

2. Describe the setting. _____
   _____

3. How did you return to the past? _____
   _____

4. Describe the past to which you returned. _____
   _____
   _____

5. You returned to the past with your knowledge of the present. Did you change anything in the past? If so, what? If not, why not? _____
   _____
   _____
   _____

6. How did any changes you made in the past affect the present and perhaps the future? _____
   _____
   _____

1.97 The Voice

Directions: Imagine that a stuffed animal, doll, or toy character suddenly began to talk. Answer the questions and write a story about this talking object. Create interesting characters, a descriptive setting, a well-defined plot, and a climax for your story.

1. Describe the main characters, including the talking object, in your story.

_____

_____

2. Describe the setting. _____

_____

3. When did the object begin to talk? _____

4. Why did it talk? _____

_____

5. What did it say? _____

_____

6. What did you do when it began to talk? _____

_____

_____

_____

7. Could anyone else hear the object talk? Why or why not? _____

_____

8. Did the object stop talking? Explain. _____

_____

Weird, Strange, and Unbelievable

1.98 Fantastic Pet

Directions: Imagine being able to have a fantastic pet—for example, a dragon, a unicorn, or a giant eagle on which you can fly to the highest mountain peak. Answer the questions and write a story about your fantastic pet. Create interesting characters, a descriptive setting, an exciting plot, and a climax for your story.

1. Describe your fantastic pet. _____
_____
_____

2. Describe the main characters in your story. _____
_____
_____

3. Describe the setting. _____
_____

4. How did you get your fantastic pet? _____
_____

5. Describe an adventure you and your fantastic pet had. _____
_____
_____
_____
_____
_____
_____

1.99 Mysterious Artifact

Directions: An *artifact* is an object that was produced long ago, such as a very old coin, tool, or ring. Imagine that you are exploring a cave and you find an ancient, mysterious artifact. Answer the questions, then write a story about this artifact and its special powers. Create interesting characters, a descriptive setting, an exciting plot, and a climax for your story.

1. Describe the main characters in your story. _____

   _____

   _____

2. Describe the setting. _____

   _____

3. Describe the artifact you found. _____

   _____

4. What are its special powers? _____

   _____

5. How did you learn of these powers? _____

   _____

6. What happened after you learned of its powers? _____

   _____

   _____

7. Did you keep the artifact? Or did you return it to the cave so that no one else could find it? Explain. _____

   _____

Weird, Strange, and Unbelievable

1.100 Super Student

Directions: Imagine that you acquire the power to correctly answer every question your teachers ask. But this power lasts only a day. Answer the questions and write a story about when you were a super student. Create interesting characters, a descriptive setting, a well-defined plot, and a climax for your story.

1. Describe the main characters in your story. _____

_____

_____

2. Describe the setting. _____

_____

3. How do you acquire super student power? _____

_____

4. How do you feel having this power? _____

_____

5. Describe what you do with this power. _____

_____

_____

_____

6. Does anyone know about your power? Explain. _____

_____

7. What happens when your power begins to weaken and you return to

   normal? _____

_____

_____

PART 2

Writing the Draft

The draft is the part of the writing process in which ideas are put into words and onto paper. For many students, this is a hard and frustrating task. It is the real work of writing.

Expressing ideas is a big step beyond conceiving ideas, and even the most capable students often need encouragement and guidance to articulate their thoughts and fashion them into a clearly written piece. To help your students approach their drafts with confidence, explain that a first draft is only the first attempt of what may turn out to be many attempts at completing a piece. Few writers get a draft "right" the first time, or the second, or the third. It is not uncommon for professional authors to work through a dozen or more drafts, and even then they may not be fully satisfied that they expressed their ideas in the best way possible. A draft should be considered as but one step forward in the writing process.

For many writers the draft is a time of discovery. Some drafts closely follow the ideas that the writer has already formulated; others lead the writer to new ideas. Some are written quickly with high energy and emotion; others are written in a series of starts and stops because the writer has trouble finding her way. Some surprise the writer with unexpected insights; others are disappointing and force the writer to return to his original ideas to figure out what is wrong. Throughout all this, it is the writer's decisions that ultimately guide the development of the draft.

Students should look at a draft as a testing ground where they can examine their ideas and decide whether they are writing exactly what they wish to say. I once had a student who expressed frustration that he had to write four drafts of a story before he was satisfied he had expressed his ideas the best he could. I explained that writing the first three drafts was the only way he could have gotten to the fourth. Rather than viewing reworked drafts as failures, students should see each draft as an opportunity that leads them closer to the clear expression of ideas.

Without question, writing a draft is work. You can, however, make writing drafts easier for your students by teaching them the basics of composition. By middle school, students should understand the fundamentals of sentences and paragraphs. It is upon these fundamentals that you can instruct your students in the skills necessary to elevate their writing from elementary expression to expression that is both compelling and effective.

Sentences: The Foundation of the Draft

To write with competence, students must have a basic knowledge and understanding of the four types of sentences—*declarative, interrogative, imperative,* and *exclamatory*—as well as the four sentence structures—*simple, compound, complex,* and *compound-complex*. Understanding sentence types and structures will help them to write with proficiency and variety.

Exercise 2.1 Types of Sentences

Write the following sample sentences on an overhead projector or the board:

- Elena studied for her history test. (declarative)
- Did Kevin complete his science project? (interrogative)
- Close the door. (imperative)
- Look out! (exclamatory)

Discuss each of the four types of sentences and point out the end punctuation. A declarative sentence is a statement and requires a period. An interrogative sentence is a question and requires a question mark. An imperative sentence is a command and requires a period. An exclamatory sentence expresses great emotion and requires an exclamation point.

Next, explain that a sentence must contain a subject and a predicate to express a complete thought. Note the subject and predicate in each of the examples. In the declarative sentence, *Elena* is the subject and *studied* is the predicate. In the interrogative sentence, *Kevin* is the subject and *did complete* is the predicate. In the imperative sentence, *close* is the predicate and the subject is understood to be *you*, the person to whom the command is directed. *You* (understood) is also the subject of the exclamatory sentence, in which *look* is the predicate.

After discussing the examples, ask students to volunteer other examples of each type of sentence. Write the examples on an overhead projector or the board and identify the subjects and predicates of the sentences. For additional practice with sentences, assign Worksheets 2.1 and 2.2 at the end of this section.

Write the following examples of sentence structures on an overhead projector or the board:

- Giorgio writes for the school newspaper. (simple)
- Tyrel enjoys baseball, but his sister prefers soccer. (compound)
- When lightning struck a pole on our street, the whole neighborhood lost power. (complex)
- Because it was spring break, Mrs. Jones did not assign homework, but she encouraged her students to continue reading their novels. (compound-complex)

Explain that English sentences can take the form of any of these four structures. Understanding these structures will help students to vary their writing. Of course, the amount of information about sentences you provide to your students should be based on their abilities and needs. Advanced students will likely benefit from more instruction on predicate nominatives, direct and indirect objects, and the different kinds of phrases, while for some students, simply realizing there are different kinds of sentences will help them to vary their writing.

The first example is a simple sentence. It has one subject, *Giorgio*, and one predicate, *writes*.

The second example is a compound sentence. In a compound sentence, two separate sentences, often referred to as *independent* or *main clauses*, are connected with coordinating conjunctions such as *and*, *but*, *or*, or *nor*. Note the subject, *Tyrel*, and the predicate, *enjoys*, in the first sentence, and the subject, *sister*, and the predicate, *prefers*, in the second. Also note that *but* is a conjunction that connects the sentences.

The third example is a complex sentence. A complex sentence has one *independent clause*, which can stand alone as a simple sentence, and at least one *dependent* (also called *subordinate*) *clause*, which cannot. In the example, "When lightning struck a pole on our street" is the dependent clause, and "the whole neighborhood lost power" is the independent clause.

The final example is a compound-complex sentence. A compound-complex sentence contains two or more independent clauses and one or more dependent clauses. The example contains one dependent clause, "Because it was spring break," and two independent clauses, "Mrs. Jones did not assign homework" and "she encouraged her students to continue reading their novels," connected by the conjunction *but*.

Emphasize to your students that by using all four forms of sentence structures they will be able to vary their writing and present their ideas in an interesting manner. Ask volunteers to offer examples of each structure. Write their examples on an overhead projector or the board and discuss them, making sure that everyone can identify each of the four forms. Depending on your class, you may need to discuss and provide additional examples of compound-complex sentences.

Write this example on an overhead projector or the board:

> *After school Olivia hurried home. She finished her homework. She went to dance practice.*

Explain that these three simple sentences, although written correctly, are flat and boring. Imagine a whole article or story written like this. Short sentences like these can be combined to make writing smoother and more interesting, as in the following example:

> *After school Olivia hurried home, finished her homework, and went to dance practice.*

Now offer this example:

> *The sun edged above the horizon. The sky brightened.*

Explain that two simple sentences such as the ones above can often be rewritten as a compound or complex sentence. Combining and rewriting these sentences slightly can result in a noteworthy difference:

> *As the sun edged above the horizon, the sky brightened.*

Emphasize that combining and varying sentences makes writing more interesting and showcases ideas for readers. For additional practice, assign Worksheets 2.3 and 2.4 at the end of this section.

Creating Paragraphs

A well-written paragraph is constructed of sentences related to one main idea. The paragraph contains a topic sentence, which states the main idea, and other sentences that support the main idea with details and examples.

Although the topic sentence is the first sentence in most paragraphs, it may appear in the middle or at the end. For most students, placing the topic sentence at the beginning of the paragraph makes it easier to organize the paragraph and provide supporting details.

Paragraphs vary in length, depending on their main idea and supporting details. When students ask you how long a paragraph should be (and they will), say that a paragraph must be long enough to fully develop its main idea.

A major problem with the paragraphs of many young writers is insufficient development. Students often use general or vague main ideas or supporting ideas that lack specific details. Encourage your students to develop their paragraphs one sentence at a time, starting with the topic sentence, which they must then support with details and examples.

Exercise 2.4 Constructing Paragraphs

Write this example of an obviously undeveloped paragraph on an overhead projector or the board:

The movie was great. It had a lot of action, and I liked the performances of the actors. It was the best movie I ever saw.

Explain that although it is clear the writer liked the movie, she offers few supporting details. The absence of supporting ideas undermines the main idea. Ask your students what kinds of details could be included that would support and strengthen the main idea in this paragraph. Write their suggestions down and discuss them, noting how they could support the main idea. Possible details include the following:

- The title of the movie
- The type of movie
- A brief description of the plot and how it helped to make the movie great
- Specific examples of the action
- Descriptions of the characters and the performances of the actors and actresses

In a well-constructed paragraph every sentence supports the main idea. Ideally, even the last sentence of a paragraph should contain an idea that either summarizes or adds a final point to the main idea and then leads into the next paragraph. The effective use of transitional words and phrases helps writing to flow smoothly, resulting in each paragraph seamlessly flowing into the next.

Exercise 2.5 Using Transitions

Write the following words on an overhead projector or the board:

- after
- although
- before
- finally
- instead of
- just as
- rather than

Explain that these terms—and others like them—are often used as *transitions* to help writing flow effortlessly from one paragraph to another.

Write the following example on an overhead projector or the board; or you may prefer to simply read the example aloud to your students:

> *The snow began falling soon after dinner and continued through the night. By the time Marta went to bed, several inches had already fallen. She figured school would be canceled tomorrow.*
>
> *Marta played all day in the snow. She and her friends went sledding, built a snowman, and had a snowball fight.*

Ask your students their opinions of these two paragraphs. Most will point out that the first changes abruptly to the second. The change is almost jarring. From Marta figuring school would be canceled the idea switches to playing in the snow. There is no transition. The reader is given no warning of the coming change, the flow is disrupted, and the writing is weakened.

Ask your students how this can be revised. Students will no doubt offer several possibilities for transitions, which you might write on the overhead projector or the board. Here is one possibility:

> *Just as she had thought, school was canceled, and the next day Marta played. . . .*

Note how the words "Just as" and "the next day" make a smooth transition between paragraphs by carrying the idea of school being canceled in the first paragraph over to the second. Suggest that your students note the use of transitions in the materials they read, as well as in their own writing.

Exercise 2.6 Reviewing Paragraphs

From your students' reading book, or their science or social studies text, choose two or three descriptive paragraphs. (Descriptive paragraphs are best for this exercise because they include details.) Have your students read the paragraphs. For each one identify the main idea, find the topic sentence, and discuss the supporting details. Direct the attention of your students to the construction of the paragraph, particularly how details support and expand the main idea. You might also wish to point out examples of smooth transitions, noting how they help one paragraph lead into another.

Encourage your students to concentrate on building solid paragraphs in their writing. Remind them to organize each paragraph around a main idea, express that idea in a topic sentence, and provide supporting details. For additional practice with paragraphs, assign Worksheets 2.5, 2.6, 2.7, and 2.8 at the end of this section.

Showing and Not Telling

Good writers understand that they must show and not tell about ideas if their writing is to have the greatest impact. Because showing requires action, authors who show and avoid merely telling write with sharper and clearer imagery. The difference between telling about an idea and showing the idea through action can be significant.

Exercise 2.7 Show, Don't Tell

To illustrate to your students the power of showing over telling, write this example on an overhead projector or the board:

- After striking out with the bases loaded, Pete's temper flared. (telling)
- After looking at a third strike with the bases loaded, Pete threw his bat down and slammed his helmet to the ground. (showing)

Explain that in the first sentence the writer tells that Pete lost control of his temper. In the second sentence, however, "threw his bat down and slammed his helmet to the ground" shows his temper flaring. Note also that "looking at a third strike" is more specific than simply striking out. Showing provides action that the reader can visualize in his imagination, making the idea clear.

Now offer this example:

- The sunset was breathtaking. (telling)
- The sun slipped below the horizon in the bright red sky. (showing)

The second sentence provides action—"The sun slipped below the horizon"—and visual details—"in the bright red sky"—that enhance the idea of the sun setting. The second sentence is an example of stronger writing than the first, because it shows rather than tells.

Ask your students to volunteer additional examples that demonstrate showing and not telling. Write the examples on an overhead projector or the board and discuss the differences between showing and telling.

Encourage your students to show and not merely tell whenever possible. For more practice, assign Worksheet 2.9 at the end of this section.

Using Adjectives and Adverbs Wisely

Many students use too many adjectives and adverbs in their writing. Some overuse these modifiers in a mistaken assumption that more details will make their writing better. The opposite is true. When overused, adjectives and adverbs weaken writing. Moreover, relying too heavily on adjectives and adverbs can cloud writing and distract the writer from choosing distinct nouns and strong verbs. Too many adjectives and adverbs result in verbose expression that plods along toward the boring. Adjectives and adverbs should be used only when necessary.

Following are some examples of overused adjectives and adverbs I have come across in the writing of my students:

- the evil, wicked, hateful witch (Most readers get the idea with "evil witch.")
- green grass (Unless the grass is dead or the season is winter, grass is green.)
- totally surprised (Can someone be partially surprised?)
- the hard granite boulder (Is granite ever soft?)
- completely fooled (A person is either fooled or not fooled.)
- happy smile (Most smiles arise from happiness; the exception is a sad smile.)

When you teach the use of adjectives and adverbs to your students, explain that these words have a purpose in sentences but must be chosen with care. Instead of bland modifiers, students should seek ones that provide sharp, distinct details, and even then they should be used only when essential to achieving precise meaning.

To help your students gain an understanding and appreciation of the use of adjectives and adverbs, note examples in their reading. Point out how the proper use of adjectives or adverbs can enhance expression and sharpen meaning. To provide your students with practice using adjectives and adverbs wisely in their writing, assign Worksheets 2.10, 2.11, and 2.12 at the end of this section.

Order and Sequence

In real life, things happen in order. All the things we do are part of a long (and sometimes complicated) sequence of cause and effect. In the same way, articles and stories must adhere to some form of order and sequence. Even stories that include flashbacks follow a plan.

For some students, the order in their writing resembles the order of a messy desk. The writing of these students can be hard to follow and certainly can be improved.

Problems with order usually arise from one of two causes: either the student is simply inattentive to order because she wants to finish the writing as quickly as possible, or the student is so enthused with expressing her ideas that attention to order is lost in the heat of writing. Whatever the reason, it must be corrected. Effective writing exhibits a sequential development of ideas in an ordered framework.

To help your students gain an understanding of order and sequence, discuss order and sequence in the stories and articles they read. Especially point out how ideas develop logically, how they are related, and how they are usually presented in sequence.

You should encourage your students to concentrate on the order of ideas in their writing. Explain that the ideas in most pieces should build coherently from start to end. For most students, either of two types of organization—a chronological pattern or a logical pattern—provides a practical order.

In a *chronological pattern*, ideas are arranged according to the way they occurred in time. For students who have trouble maintaining a coherent order in their writing, suggest that they write a list of their ideas according to time. Referring to their list as they write will help them adhere to an accurate sequence.

In a *logical pattern*, ideas are arranged according to specific criteria. For example, ideas may be arranged from least to most important, or most to least important. Descriptions may be detailed from outside to inside or inside to outside, top to bottom or bottom to top. A logical organizational pattern may take a variety of forms, provided the pattern is reasonable and consistent.

Encourage your students to consider various plans when they are organizing material for writing. Their most important consideration should be to organize their material in a manner that presents their ideas clearly to readers. To provide students with practice on order and sequence, assign Worksheet 2.13 at the end of this section.

Exercise 2.8 Organizational Plans

On an overhead projector or the board, write the following two organizational plans:

- **Chronological pattern.** According to time. What happens first comes first. What happens second comes next. What happens third comes next, and so on.
- **Logical pattern.** According to specific criteria. Ideas may be arranged in various ways, provided they follow a clear pattern.

Ask your students to suggest ideas that would best be described in each pattern. For example, a narrative of a camping trip should probably be organized in a chronological pattern, while an essay about the causes of the Revolutionary War might be best organized in a logical pattern of most to least important factors.

Encourage your students to identify the organization of material they read. Ask them to note which they find more often—the chronological pattern or the logical pattern.

Using Active Constructions

Active constructions, sometimes referred to as *active voice*, help to make writing direct and strong. Passive constructions, also known as *passive voice*, make writing indirect and weak. Active constructions are clear and add force to writing. There is nothing vague or ambiguous about an active construction, as the following example shows:

- Taryn scored the winning goal. (active)
- The winning goal was scored by Taryn. (passive)

Notice that the active construction is shorter and provides a clear idea. The passive construction muddles along. In the active construction, *Taryn* is the subject and *scored* is the predicate. There is no confusion that Taryn scored the goal. In the passive construction, *goal* is the subject and the predicate is the phrase *was scored*. *Taryn* becomes the object of the preposition *by*. Most readers easily understand the first sentence; some, however, have to think a little about the second. Active constructions are almost always a better choice than passive constructions, because they help readers to visualize action and ideas.

Exercise 2.9 Choosing Active Constructions

Write the following example on an overhead projector or the board:

- Jamal kicked a field goal. (active)
- A field goal was kicked by Jamal. (passive)

Explain to your students the differences between active and passive constructions. Note that in the first sentence the action is clear. Although the second sentence says the same thing, it does not express the action as clearly as the first. Emphasize that this is the major difference between active and passive constructions: Active constructions are clear and direct; passive constructions are wordy and less clear.

If necessary, offer this example:

- Larissa cuddled the puppy. (active)
- The puppy was cuddled by Larissa. (passive)

Ask your students which sentence they prefer. All (or at least most) should prefer the first, which is the active construction. For practice with active and passive constructions, assign Worksheet 2.14 at the end of this section.

Choosing Strong Verbs

Closely linked to active constructions are strong verbs. Like active constructions, strong verbs paint clear pictures in the imaginations of readers. English is a vast, rich language. We have words for just about everything, and we have precise verbs for all kinds of action. Encouraging your students to use precise action verbs in their writing will help them to master this important writing technique.

Exercise 2.10 Strong Verbs

Write the following pairs of sentences on an overhead projector or the board:

> The wind was blowing hard through the night.
> The wind howled through the night.
>
> The squirrel went from branch to branch.
> The squirrel scampered from branch to branch.
>
> The little boy cried loudly during his tantrum.
> The little boy shrieked during his tantrum.

Explain that the second sentence of each pair uses a strong verb to show the action. Strong verbs are clear in the action they express. They result in writing that is less wordy, particularly in cases where adverbs are used to support a verb's action. For practice with strong verbs, assign Worksheet 2.15 at the end of this section.

Verb Tenses

The tense of a verb shows when something happens, happened, or will happen in a sentence. The three most commonly used tenses are *present*, *past*, and *future*. Middle school students should also understand *present perfect*, *past perfect*, and *future perfect* tenses.

Explain to your students what each tense shows:

• Verbs in the present tense show action that is happening now. For example, *Sandra talks with Lisa each day.*
• Verbs in the past tense show action that has happened. *Sandra talked to Lisa yesterday.*
• Verbs in the future tense show action that will happen. *Sandra will talk to Lisa tomorrow.*
• Verbs in the present perfect tense show action that has been completed in the past and might be continuing in the present. Such verbs require *has* or *have* with the past participle. *Sandra has talked with Lisa.*

- Verbs in the past perfect tense show past action that ended before another past action began. Such verbs require *had* with the past participle. *Sandra had talked with Lisa.*
- Verbs in the future perfect tense show a future action that will have ended before another action begins. Such verbs require *shall have* or *will have* with the past participle. *Sandra will have talked with Lisa.*

Explain to your students that most writers use the past tense more than any other tense because the events they are writing about have already happened. This is especially true for stories and most articles. In some articles, however—for example, essays and editorials—an author may want to convey a feeling that the subject of the article is currently happening. In such cases, the author uses present tense.

As you discuss tenses with your students, note that they must choose the correct tense for the stories and articles they write. A narrative based on a past event requires the past tense. An article about the lunches currently served in the school cafeteria would probably best be written in the present tense. Much of an article that speculates about the end of the current school year should probably be written in the future tense.

Once a tense is chosen, consistency is essential. Encourage your students to pay close attention to the tenses they use to avoid shifting tenses unnecessarily. I have read pieces in which students start in the past tense, then switch to the present, only to switch back to the past. Tense shifts often occur when students write action scenes in stories. They become so involved with the action, which in their imaginations is immediate, that they inadvertently switch from the past to the present tense. Once the action scene is done, they return to the past.

Selecting an inappropriate tense for writing and unnecessarily shifting tenses prove to be confusing for readers. Tense shifts can undermine expression and obscure ideas. For practice with verb tenses, assign Worksheet 2.16 at the end of this section.

Subject-Verb Agreement

A subject and verb of a sentence must always agree in number. Singular subjects require the singular form of verbs in the present tense, and plural subjects require the plural form of verbs. Agreement is not an issue for sentences in the past tense, because in the past tense, except for the verb *be*, the forms of verbs are the same for singular and plural subjects. (In the past tense, the verb *be* assumes either of two forms: *was* or *were*.)

Exercise 2.11 Agreement Issues of Subjects and Verbs

On an overhead projector or the board, write the following examples:

- Tina rides the bus to school each day.
- Tina and Samantha ride the bus to school each day.
- Tina rode the bus to school yesterday.
- Tina and Samantha rode the bus to school yesterday.

Discuss the sentences and point out the subjects and verbs. Note that in the present tense, students must pay close attention to subject–verb agreement. In the present tense, the singular subject *Tina* requires the singular form of the verb *ride*, which is *rides*, and the plural subjects *Tina* and *Samantha* require the plural form *ride*. When using the past tense, both singular and plural subjects use the same form, *rode*. For additional practice with subject–verb agreement, assign Worksheet 2.17 at the end of this section.

Using Point of View Correctly

Point of view (POV) is the perspective an author uses to tell a story or write an article. The two most common points of view are the *first person point of view* and the *third person point of view*. Virtually all of your students will use these two points of view in their writing.

In the first person POV, the author participates in or observes the action. The author tells the story or writes about an event or issue firsthand and refers to himself as *I*. Students often find the first person POV easier to write with because they can use their own voices. It is also easier to write with emotion and feeling in the first person POV, because the writer assumes a role in the piece. The major disadvantage of this POV is the way in which it limits writing, especially for stories. The author, as participant in and narrator of the story, can write only about what she experiences in the story. For example, while writing in the first person POV, the author cannot describe the thoughts or feelings of another character (unless the author reads minds).

In the third person POV, the author writes from a perspective outside the piece. The author is not a part of the action. Characters are referred to as *he* or *she*. The third person POV allows the author broader control of the piece, but the writing may not have the intimacy of a piece written in the first person. Most writing is done in the third person POV.

Probably the biggest problem students have with POV is consistency. Students may start a story in the first person, switch to third, then switch back to first, only to switch once again to third. Rapid or unexpected switches between first and third person befuddle readers, and often confuse the writer as well. Stories and articles that suffer from unnecessary POV switches quickly lose focus. Ideas become muddled and writing loses direction.

You might wish to explain to your students that some stories use third person multiple POV characters. In such stories, the POV changes from character to character to give readers a different perspective for the story; however, the POV shifts usually occur at the beginning of scenes or chapters.

Exercise 2.12 Identifying Point of View

Write the following example on an overhead projector or the board:

> *I had a busy day. I had two tests in school, had band practice after school, and had to finish my history report after dinner.*

Ask your students to identify the POV in the example. Obviously, it is the first person. Now ask volunteers to change the POV from the first person to the third person. Students might substitute *John* or *Jen* or *he* or *she* for *I*; however, they would also have to change *my* to *his* or *her*.

Review the advantages and disadvantages of each POV and warn your students to be careful of shifting POV unnecessarily. To help your students gain an understanding of POV, discuss examples in their reading and explore why authors chose the POV they did.

As your students learn to recognize POV in their reading, they will use it effectively in their writing. For practice with POV, assign Worksheets 2.18 and 2.19 at the end of this section.

Using Comparison and Contrast

Comparing and contrasting are tools that enable writers to identify similarities and differences. They allow writers to highlight details that evoke powerful images. Comparing and contrasting help to delineate ideas.

Explain to your students that comparing identifies similarities and that contrasting identifies differences. They should use comparison and contrast whenever they need to show how two things or ideas are alike and different.

Note that there are two methods for comparing and contrasting. In the first method, the author describes the first idea fully and then describes the second fully, showing how they are alike and different. In the second method, the author describes one feature of the first idea and compares and contrasts it to the same feature of the second idea. The author then compares and contrasts the second feature, then the third, and so on. Either method enables writers to draw clear distinctions between ideas.

Exercise 2.13 Comparing and Contrasting Pets

On an overhead projector or the board, write "cat" and "dog," or similar topics students are likely to be familiar with. Explain to your students that the class is going to compare and contrast cats and dogs.

Ask your students to volunteer ideas how cats and dogs are alike and different. Some similarities might include the following:

- Both animals are mammals.
- Both are popular as pets.
- As pets they can become "members of the family."

Differences students might suggest include the following:

- Dogs are more playful; cats like to "do their own thing."
- Cats purr when contented; dogs wag their tails.
- Cats meow; dogs bark.

These are just some possibilities, and it is likely your students will come up with more. Suggest that students use comparing and contrasting in their own writing. For additional practice with comparison and contrast, assign Worksheet 2.20 at the end of this section.

Using Figurative Language

Figurative language can turn average writing into exceptional writing. Figures of speech include *similes*, *metaphors*, and *personification*.

Explain to your students that similes make comparisons using the words *like*, *as*, or *than*. Metaphors make comparisons without using these signal words. Personification gives human qualities to nonhuman things and ideas. The great power of figurative language manifests in the enrichment of ideas.

Exercise 2.14 The Power of Figures of Speech

Write the following examples of figures of speech on an overhead projector or the board:

- The clown's happy grin was like a half moon. (simile)
- Bart's blue eyes were as cold as ice. (simile)
- He was slier than a fox. (simile)

- The fog was a shroud over the valley. (metaphor)
- The birds sang their morning melodies. (personification)

Discuss each of the examples and note how the comparison or personification is made. Also discuss how the figures of speech help readers to visualize the idea expressed by the sentence. Ask your students to volunteer examples of similes, metaphors, and personifications. Write them down and discuss them, noting how the figures of speech enrich the ideas of sentences. For additional practice, assign Worksheet 2.21 at the end of this section.

Using Symbols

A *symbol* is something that has meaning beyond itself. Authors employ symbolism to give a character, object, place, or idea greater meaning that it normally has.

Explain to your students that symbolism is apparent throughout society. For example, a flag is a symbol of a country, a tree may be a symbol for conservation, and a sunrise may be a symbol for a new beginning.

Exercise 2.15 Using Symbolism Effectively

To give your students practice in recognizing symbolism, write the following symbols on an overhead projector or the board:

- Light
- Darkness
- Chain
- Eagle
- Fox

Ask your students what each might represent. Light, for example, might represent knowledge or wisdom; darkness might represent evil or trouble; a chain might represent being held back in some way; an eagle might represent power or freedom; and a fox might represent slyness.

Encourage your students to use symbolism when appropriate in their writing. For additional practice with symbolism, assign Worksheet 2.22 at the end of this section.

Reproducible Worksheets

For many students, writing the draft is the most difficult part of the writing process. The worksheets included in this section are designed to give students practice in the techniques and strategies that make writing a draft easier. The skills covered on the worksheets are the foundation of proficient writing. Encourage your students to incorporate these skills in their writing.

The worksheets that follow are linked to the teaching suggestions of this part of the book. While each worksheet stands alone and can be assigned with little or no introduction, the worksheets will be most effective if you offer instruction and guidance on the skills presented. Once the skills have been taught, reinforce them through the revision process that is described in Part 3.

2.1 Kinds of Sentences

Directions: Follow the instructions and write examples of the four kinds of sentences. Be sure to use correct end punctuation.

1. Write a declarative sentence using each of the following.

A. eagle _____

_____

B. weather _____

_____

2. Write an interrogative sentence using each of the following.

A. movie _____

_____

B. dinner _____

_____

3. Write an imperative sentence using each of the following.

A. door _____

B. homework _____

4. Write an exclamatory sentence using each of the following.

A. step _____

B. truck _____

2.2 Expanding Sentences

Directions: Expand each sentence by adding words, phrases, or clauses.

1. The wolf howled. _____

_____

2. Riley stubbed his toe. _____

_____

3. Deanna searched everywhere. _____

_____

4. Nikki finished. _____

_____

5. The storm raged. _____

_____

6. Raphael rushed to his bus stop. _____

_____

7. Katie performed. _____

_____

8. The river spilled over its banks. _____

_____

9. Madison waited for her mother. _____

_____

10. Sean grinned. _____

_____

Writing the Draft

2.3 Combining Sentences

1. Carl mowed the lawn. He trimmed the hedges. _____

_____

2. It rained all day. The soccer game was postponed. _____

_____

3. Maria and Melinda are twins. They don't look much like each other.

_____

4. The evening grew darker. The stars soon appeared. _____

_____

5. Mandy plays soccer. She plays softball, too. _____

_____

6. We might go to a movie. We might go shopping instead. _____

_____

7. Juan had to do his history report. He had to finish his math homework

   first. _____

_____

8. The kitten crept up on the toy mouse. It pounced on the mouse.

_____

Writing the Draft

2.4 Varying Sentences

Directions: Rewrite each sentence. Use the given word or phrase to vary the form of the sentence. The first one is done as an example.

1. The sun rose and the morning brightened. (as) *As the sun rose, the morning brightened.*

2. LuAnn finished her science assignment, and then she started her math. (after) _____

3. It snowed heavily all night, and the roads were impassable. (because) _____

4. The power went off last night, and Rob realized he did not have a flashlight. (when) _____

5. Carla had a sprained ankle, but she still went to soccer practice. (even though) _____

6. The sky became overcast, and the rain began. (once) _____

7. Trish was home with a cold, and she finished reading *Dicey's Song*. (while) _____

8. It was the middle of the night, and strange sounds woke Regina. (during) _____

Writing the Draft

2.5 Understanding Paragraphs

If you sometimes wonder what the difference is between a meteoroid, meteor, and meteorite, you are not alone. Many people find these words confusing. Meteoroids are rocky chunks of matter that hurtle through space. While many are the size of a small stone, others may be hundreds of feet wide. Most meteoroids orbit the sun and never approach Earth. Some, however, have orbits that intersect the orbit of the Earth. If these meteoroids come too close, they may be captured by the Earth's gravity and pulled into the Earth's atmosphere. Friction with the molecules in the atmosphere will cause the meteoroid to heat up and disintegrate. When a meteoroid begins to burn in the atmosphere, it leaves a streak of light. It is now called a meteor, often mistakenly referred to as a shooting star. Although most meteors disintegrate completely before they hit the ground, some make it through the atmosphere and smash into the Earth. A meteor that hits the Earth is called a meteorite. If a meteor is big, the impact will result in a great explosion and terrible destruction. Fortunately, most meteoroids remain far from the Earth. Of those that enter the atmosphere, most disintegrate long before reaching the ground.

_____

_____

_____

_____

_____

Writing the Draft

2.6 Writing Topic Sentences

1. _____

He looked at the huge pile of books on his desk. His history text, math workbook, and several notebooks waited for him. Leon had so much to do that he didn't know where to start. But he realized that if he was to finish his homework tonight, he had better begin right now.

2. _____

Although he plays many different kinds of video games, Jon likes fantasy games with wizards and brave warriors the best. He enjoys the fantastic settings and action of these games.

3. _____

She sings in her school's chorus and plays flute in the band. She also takes piano and dance lessons. On top of all this, Jenna is teaching herself how to play the guitar.

4. _____

First she looked on her desk. That was where she usually put her homework. But her book report wasn't there. Next Christy checked the family room, thinking she might have left it by the computer. It wasn't there either. About to give up, she remembered she had put the report in her knapsack last night. Now, if she could only find her knapsack.

Choose one of the paragraphs. Explain what clues helped you to decide on the topic sentence.

_____

_____

_____

_____

Writing the Draft

2.7 Using Smooth Transitions

Directions: Write a transition to connect each pair of paragraphs.

1. Marta was running late for school again. She gulped the last of her cereal and finished her glass of orange juice. Grabbing her backpack and calling good-bye to her mom, she rushed out the door.

_____

Relieved she had not missed her bus, Marta climbed aboard and plopped down on the seat.

2. The dark clouds gathering in the western sky looked ominous. Billy began walking faster. As the wind started to gust, he hoped he would get home before the storm arrived.

_____

He ran up the steps to the front door and stepped inside. He was soaked.

3. Roberta read the instructions for installing the new software for her computer. This should be simple enough, she thought. She placed the CD into the drive. Nothing happened.

_____

She examined the CD closely. Flipping it over, she placed it back in the drive.

4. Mark looked at the tools, boxes, and junk that filled Mr. White's garage. There was barely enough room to walk. He frowned, remembering his brother warning him to look inside the garage before telling Mr. White he would clean it out for $20. But he couldn't go back on his word.

_____

He carried out the boxes closest to the door first. As he continued to work, he tried to look on the bright side. He would certainly be done by the end of the week.

© Gary Robert Muschla

2.8 Writing Supporting Details

Directions: Write at least three supporting details for each topic sentence.

1. The darkening sky and growing wind promised a big storm.

_____

_____

_____

_____

2. Caroline hurried about preparing for the surprise party for her parents.

_____

_____

_____

_____

3. Becky enjoyed babysitting Mrs. Hanson's twins.

_____

_____

_____

_____

4. The drought was the worst in years.

_____

_____

_____

_____

Writing the Draft

2.9 Showing and Not Telling

1. Kevin felt miserable with a cold. _Kevin's body ached, his head hurt, and he had been sneezing and coughing all day._

2. It rained hard. _____

_____

3. Aunt Loretta is always cheerful. _____

_____

4. Christina is an excellent student. _____

_____

5. After the heavy rain, the current of the river was strong. _____

_____

6. Lisa was frightened by the noises outside the front door. _____

_____

7. Martin is an outstanding basketball player. _____

_____

8. It was a terrible storm. _____

_____

Writing the Draft

2.10 Choosing Adjectives

Directions: Complete each sentence by filling in the blank with an adjective. Choose adjectives from the list below that help to paint a distinct picture in the reader's imagination. (Not all of the adjectives will be used; a few may be used in more than one sentence.)

1. The _____ blast of the smoke detector ripped Jimmy from sleep.

2. A _____ moat surrounded the _____ castle.

3. Shari looked at the _____ computer screen and realized her report was lost.

4. All of the campers listened as the _____ man told of the _____ spirits that inhabited the surrounding woods.

5. A _____ oak tree stood at the center of the yard.

6. The _____ kitten pounced on the _____ toy mouse.

7. Jason loves _____ activities such as hiking and rock climbing.

8. The _____ mountains poked into the _____ sky.

9. As he walked home from school, Tim pulled up his collar to block the _____ wind.

10. The _____ sun scorched the desert with heat.

Adjectives

blank	invincible	wintry	playful	blazing	deep
piercing	frightening	cloudless	outdoor	mighty	fluffy
towering	physical	old	exciting	strange	empty

Writing the Draft

2.11 Choosing Adverbs

1. Travis prepared _____ for the math test and got a perfect score.

2. James _____ is a gentleman.

3. Caitlyn _____ downloaded new virus protection software for her computer.

4. The winds of the storm blew _____ through the night.

5. Nathan's little brother believed the ghost story _____.

6. Kim performed her dance routine _____ at the recital.

7. _____ it would be time to leave for the concert.

8. Not wanting to be late for the start of the movie, Casey ate his dinner _____.

9. Melissa enjoys math and finishes her math homework _____.

10. Jacob double-checked his answers on the test _____ and got every problem right.

Adverbs

recently	often	soon	carelessly	intensely
quickly	always	softly	very	easily
completely	flawlessly	thoroughly	carefully	suddenly

2.12 Writing Descriptions

Directions: Choose a place or thing you know, or create a scene in your imagination. For example, this might be the street in front of your home, a big tree in your backyard, a shopping mall, or a scene in your favorite video game or book. Think of your senses and list words that describe this place, thing, or scene. Then write a descriptive paragraph about your topic.

Place, thing, or scene: _____

1. Sight words: _____

2. Sound words: _____

3. Touch words: _____

4. Smell words: _____

5. Taste words: _____

Paragraph

_____
_____
_____
_____
_____
_____
_____
_____
_____
_____

Writing the Draft

2.13 Understanding the Order of Ideas

Directions: Each set of sentences below belongs to a paragraph. But the sentences are out of order and do not follow one another correctly. Rewrite each of the paragraphs so that the ideas are in order. Use a separate sheet of paper.

1. But she still felt nervous. Kim was nervous and could not stop fidgeting. She took a deep breath to steady herself and assumed her starting position on the floor. When her coach called her name, Kim stepped forward. When Carrie, her friend, tried to assure her that she would do fine, Kim smiled. This was her first gymnastics competition, and she was afraid she would make mistakes and let her team down.

2. He got home from practice around 4:00 P.M. He knew it was going to be an extremely busy day. After dinner Michael did research for his history project. He watched his younger brother until dinner because his parents had not yet returned from shopping. That morning, he helped his father mow the lawn and trim the hedges. By the time Michael went to sleep that night, he was exhausted. Michael woke up early on Saturday. Right after lunch Michael went to soccer practice.

2.14 Using Active Constructions

Directions: Each sentence is a passive construction. Rewrite each to make it an active construction. The first one is done as an example.

1. The Frisbee was caught by David. _David caught the Frisbee._

2. The great oak tree was uprooted by the wind. _____

   _____

3. The art club's new logo was designed by Megan. _____

   _____

4. The debate was won by Trish. _____

   _____

5. The car was washed by Tony. _____

   _____

6. A violin solo in the eighth-grade winter concert was played by Marissa.

   _____

7. The unsuspecting rabbit was crept up on by the fox. _____

   _____

8. Treacherous whiteout conditions were caused by the intense snowstorm.

   _____

9. *The Slave Dancer* was written by Paula Fox. _____

   _____

10. Homework for the spring break was assigned by Mrs. Carter. _____

    _____

Writing the Draft

2.15 Using Strong Verbs

Directions: Each sentence below uses a weak verb and an adverb to show action. Rewrite the sentences, replacing the weak verb and adverb with a strong verb of your own. The first one is done as an example.

1. The little boy quickly took the wrapping paper off his birthday present.

   The little boy ripped the wrapping paper off his birthday present.

2. The hawk was high over the field in search of prey. _____

   _____

3. The cat walked quietly toward the bird. _____

   _____

4. The girls talked softly in the library. _____

   _____

5. Joanna moved quickly out of the way of the speeding car. _____

   _____

6. The little boy cried loudly when he stubbed his toe. _____

   _____

7. Thomas went hurriedly to catch the bus before it pulled away.

   _____

8. Alvaro ran very fast to the finish line. _____

   _____

9. The cold winter wind blew intensely across the open field. _____

   _____

10. The fog was entirely over the valley. _____

   _____

2.16 Using Verb Tenses Correctly

Directions: Identify the tense used in each of the following sentences—present, past, future, present perfect, past perfect, or future perfect.

1. Liz babysits her neighbor's little girl each day after school. _____

2. Paulo will have finished reading his novel by Friday. _____

3. Michael is a great musician. _____

4. Alison walked to the park with Monica this morning. _____

5. Matt has called about the lost tickets several times. _____

6. The ventriloquist will be the final act in the show. _____

7. The dog chased the cat up a tree. _____

8. Lee Ann had asked to be excused from last week's meeting. _____

9. Bobby will study for his history test after dinner. _____

10. I predict the Cougars will win the championship by ten points.

    _____

Write a sentence of your own for each of the six tenses of verbs.

1. _____

2. _____

3. _____

4. _____

5. _____

6. _____

Writing the Draft

2.17 Making Sure Subjects and Verbs Agree

Directions: Complete each sentence by writing the correct form of a verb. Choose the verbs from the bottom of the page. Each verb should be used only once. (Remember to use the correct form of each verb.)

1. Tia _____ the best chocolate cake I have ever tasted.

2. Alexis _____ her cell phone for making calls, taking pictures, and connecting to the Internet.

3. Most kids of middle school age _____ far too much TV each day.

4. Jannie and Kim _____ several times each week to keep physically fit.

5. A family of raccoons _____ in a big tree behind our house.

6. Mark _____ football, basketball, and baseball for our school.

7. Lena _____ her younger sister with homework every evening after dinner.

8. The members of the jazz band _____ the drums each morning before classes begin.

9. Stars _____ the brightest on clear winter nights.

10. After every heavy rain the river behind the soccer fields _____ above its banks.

Verbs

play	twinkle	bake	rise	help
jog	use	watch	live	practice

146

2.18 Understanding First Person Point of View

Directions: Rewrite the story from the third person point of view to the first person point of view. Pay close attention to the use of pronouns.

Danny sighed, thinking of all the math and science homework he had to do. He also had to read another chapter in his novel.

He looked at the pile of books on his desk and frowned. He couldn't decide which book to open first, but he knew he had better start if he wanted to meet his friends later.

Danny opened his math book and began. After he finished ten word problems, he answered his science questions. Finally he read the chapter in his novel.

As soon as he was done, Danny went to see his friends, who were waiting for him at the basketball court. By the time he arrived, they had already chosen teams. They had saved a spot for Danny.

_____
_____
_____
_____
_____
_____
_____
_____
_____
_____
_____
_____
_____

Writing the Draft

2.19 Understanding Third Person Point of View

Directions: Rewrite the story from the first person point of view to the third person point of view. Pay close attention to the use of pronouns.

I woke up early on the Saturday of the five-kilometer race. My father and I would be running to help raise money for charity. I had been jogging with him four times a week for the last several weeks, and I was certain I would finish the race.

Once the race began, though, I wasn't so sure. There were a lot of hills, and we were running into the wind. I began to worry that I would become tired and have to walk to the finish line.

Remembering my father's advice about keeping a slow but steady pace, I kept going. When at last I saw the finish line, I smiled and sprinted the last hundred yards.

I didn't win any trophy. But that was OK. I was satisfied simply having run and finished my first big race.

_____

_____

_____

_____

_____

_____

_____

_____

_____

_____

_____

Writing the Draft

2.20 Using Comparison and Contrast

Directions: Read the article about African elephants and Indian elephants. List how they are alike and different.

The elephant is the largest living land mammal on Earth. There are two species of elephants: the African elephant and the Indian elephant. Both elephants have trunks and eat mostly grass and leaves. But there are important differences between the two.

The African elephant is found primarily in the tropical forests and grasslands of Africa. It is the larger of the two kinds of elephants and can reach a height of thirteen feet. It is tallest at the shoulder. The African elephant also has larger ears, which may reach a length of five feet from top to bottom. The skin of an African elephant is more wrinkled than the skin of an Indian elephant. Both male and female African elephants have tusks.

The Indian elephant is found in India and Southeast Asia. It is usually smaller than the African elephant and is tallest at the arch of the back. Only male Indian elephants have tusks.

Compare

How the African elephant and Indian elephant are alike:

_____

_____

_____

_____

Contrast

How the African elephant and Indian elephant are different:

_____

_____

_____

_____

Writing the Draft

2.21 Using Figures of Speech

Directions: Write a sentence that includes a simile for each of the following. Be sure to use *like* for a simile in one of your sentences, *as* in another, and *than* in the third.

1. eagle: _____

_____

2. thief: _____

_____

3. rocket: _____

_____

Write a sentence that includes a metaphor for each of the following.

4. alarm: _____

_____

5. shark: _____

_____

6. flowers: _____

_____

Write a sentence that includes a personification for each of the following.

7. fireflies: _____

_____

8. sky: _____

_____

2.22 Using the Power of Symbolism

Directions: Match the symbol with the idea it could represent. Write the idea on the line after the symbol.

1. door _____   a beginning

2. fire _____   a journey

3. wall _____   slyness

4. darkness _____   a passageway or opening

5. dawn _____   wisdom

6. owl _____   sadness, worry, concern

7. ship _____   knowledge, enlightenment

8. circle _____   infinity, endlessness

9. night _____   obstacle, hindrance

10. fox _____   end, finish

Choose one of the symbols above (or one of your own) and write a paragraph showing how the symbol can be used.

_____

_____

_____

_____

_____

_____

Writing the Draft

PART 3

Revision

Revision is the stage of the writing process in which an author reworks, refines, and finalizes her ideas. It is a time of "re-seeing" what she has written and making it better.

Revision is essential for improving writing, yet students often resist revision. They may feel that once they have finished the draft the writing is done; they may believe that they have written their best on the draft; or they may be unsure of how to revise. But effective revision is critical for making writing as clear and meaningful to readers as possible. For most authors, it is solid revision that leads to the successful expression of ideas. It is through revision that authors achieve their best work.

What Is Revision?

In its broadest sense, revision includes any activity that makes a draft better. In its narrowest, it is replacing one word with another because the second word better communicates what the author wants to say. Note that editing of mechanics—capitalization and punctuation, for example—also occurs during revision. However, revision should not be confused with proofreading, the primary purpose of which is to correct errors in mechanics (see Part 4, "Proofreading").

Revision includes a variety of activities. As your students revise their writing, they may be engaged in any of the following:

- Rereading
- Rewriting
- Reviewing
- Rethinking
- Rearranging
- Restructuring
- Tightening
- Deleting

- Moving
- Expanding
- Unifying
- Correcting
- Redrafting
- Checking

When you introduce revision to your students, explain that writing is not finished until it has been revised. Emphasize that all professional writers revise their work. You might mention this tidbit about Ernest Hemingway: During an interview for the *Paris Review*, Hemingway said that he rewrote the last page of his book *A Farewell to Arms* thirty-nine times before he was satisfied with his work. Undoubtedly many students' eyes will widen at that, and you might want to assure them that you do not expect them to revise their work so extensively. But this example does illustrate the seriousness with which professional authors undertake the task of revision. They know that their finest writing takes form during revision.

Nurturing Skills in Revision

Revision is detailed, demanding work. Not only must the writer work to improve specifics—for example, select the best words to express an idea clearly and smoothly—he must also work to improve the piece as a whole. Moreover, each piece is different and has different strengths and weaknesses. For most authors, revision is a process that is a varying mix of art, craft, and effort.

Although just about every article or story benefits from revision, the amount and type of revision vary. Some pieces require extensive revision. Maybe the writer drifted off the topic, maybe he did not provide enough information to explain his ideas, or maybe his organization was weak. Perhaps his use of metaphors was lacking, or he used too many weak verbs and passive constructions. In other cases, a piece might require only some tightening and minor rewriting. Explain to your students that the author's initial task during revision is to recognize what needs to be reworked and what does not.

Being able to recognize what needs to be revised requires a grasp of the fundamentals of effective writing (which were discussed in Part 2, "Writing the Draft"). The following elements are essential to any piece and will provide your students with direction as they revise their writing. Depending on the abilities of your students, you might find it useful to review these elements in some detail:

- Effective, logical organization
- Basic structure of opening, body, and closing
- Well-constructed paragraphs
- Main ideas and supporting details and examples
- Varied sentence structure

- Agreement of subjects and verbs
- Active constructions
- Strong verbs
- Showing and not telling
- Consistent tenses
- Consistent point of view
- Smooth flow and effective transitions
- Figurative language
- Symbolism

When teaching revision, base your expectations for revision only on skills that you have taught. Focus on one or two skills at a time, because addressing too many at once can be overwhelming to students. You must also adjust your instruction to the level and abilities of your students. Use terminology your students understand and that provides guidance. Avoid vague terms that offer little direction, such as "insufficient development," "inconsistent," and "requires clarification." Instead, offer clear suggestions and comments that address specific weaknesses, for example, "incorrect tense shift from past to present." Such notations can help students quickly identify the weaknesses in their writing.

For many students, revision can be both puzzling and frustrating. Many work hard on a draft—feeling they wrote the best they could—and once the draft is finished, they do not know how they can make it better. To improve their writing, they need guidance and encouragement.

Although you should offer as much guidance and encouragement as you can for revision, be mindful not to revise for your students. Sometimes students will be stumped in trying to revise a part of their writing and will ask you for help. When they do, avoid making the changes for them. You can offer suggestions, for example, "What else might you say that can help your readers visualize this scene?" or "What more do you think your readers will want to know about this?" or "How might you make this more exciting?" But leave the actual changes to your students.

Revision is an individual process, based on the writer's purpose for the piece. Thus, decisions for revision are the responsibility of the author. When students revise their own work, they grow as writers.

A Plan for Revision

Because revision encompasses so many elements, there is no firm, set procedure for revising one's writing. As they gain experience with revision, most writers eventually develop their own methods. But this takes time. Practice leads to proficiency, but until they master the skills necessary for effective revision, your students need your instruction and support.

To help your students with their revision efforts, encourage them to start revising from the perspective of the overall piece and work down to the details. This plan provides direction and helps students to focus on specific elements at different points in the revision process.

Instruct your students to begin by reading through the piece and concentrating on unity. *Unity* is a broad term that can be used to include virtually all aspects of a piece. In the early grades unity may be limited to refer to topic and theme, but by middle school the idea of unity should cover the major features of a student's writing.

In an article or story that demonstrates unity, all parts work together to create effective expression. All main ideas and supporting details relate to the topic. Everything moves the piece forward in support of the author's purpose and theme. For example, an article about how to study for tests that drifts and includes information about the pleasure of reading would suffer from a lack of unity. It would prove to be confusing to readers, who expect to learn about test-taking strategies and not about reading for enjoyment. To achieve unity, any material not essential to the topic should be deleted.

The style of writing, including the use of figures of speech and symbolism, also contributes to (or detracts) from unity. Style helps to determine the mood of a piece. For example, a horror story should be written in a dark, foreboding style, which can result in a suspenseful mood; and a humorous essay should be written in an easy style that generates a lighthearted mood. A style that does not suit the topic weakens the impact of the writer's ideas.

After making certain that all parts of the piece belong, and that the writing shows unity, students should read through the piece again and concentrate on the overall structure. There should be a solid opening, logical development through the body, and a strong closing. The introduction should lead into the body, and the body should lead into the closing. Paragraphs should be used to develop main ideas, and main ideas should be supported with details and examples. Moreover, the various parts of the piece should be in balance. Ideas of equal importance should be given equal weight; ideas of lesser importance should be given less weight. All parts of the piece should complement each other.

Next, students should focus on consistency of tense. Throughout the piece, all tenses should be consistent and appropriate. For example, a story should be written in the past tense. An essay, however, might best be written in the present. Any unnecessary shifts in tense should be corrected.

Point of view must be consistent as well. If a story is started in the first person point of view, it should continue in the first person. Likewise, if a story is begun in the third person point of view, it should remain in the third person. Switching from first to third person point of view weakens a piece and undermines the author's control of the material.

After focusing on general consistency, your students should concentrate on individual paragraphs, sentences, phrases, and words. Again, they should eliminate anything that does not belong. They should strive to ensure that every expository paragraph has a topic sentence and sufficient details. In addition, encourage students to vary and combine sentences, make certain that subjects and verbs agree, rely on active constructions, and select just the right words to express their ideas.

Figures of speech—similes, metaphors, and personification—and symbolism should be appropriate for the topic and enhance expression. Now is the time to make writing the best it can be.

As students gain experience and confidence in revision, most will revise weaknesses as they go along, addressing various elements of their writing simultaneously. They will come to see revision as a satisfying part of the writing process because it enables them to make certain that their writing expresses exactly what they wish to say.

Exercise 3.1 Revision Plan for Students

On an overhead projector or the board, write the following steps of a revision plan for your students:

1. Read the entire piece and focus on unity—all parts should relate to the whole.
2. Focus on writing style—make sure it creates the right mood for the topic.
3. Focus on structure—opening, body, and closing. Main ideas should be developed with details and examples.
4. Focus on consistency of tense.
5. Focus on consistency of point of view.
6. Focus on individual paragraphs, sentences, phrases, and words—all should help to express ideas clearly.

Discuss these steps with your students. Explain that revision often requires rereading and reworking writing several times. Following a basic plan that concentrates on looking at the overall piece and working down through the details can be a helpful strategy.

Exercise 3.2 Recognizing Good Writing

Recognizing good writing of others is a major step in revising one's own writing. Use well-written articles and stories from your students' texts as examples and discuss why these pieces may be viewed as samples of good writing. Read the material and note the unity, how everything in the article or story relates to the topic and the author's purpose. Note the organization of the piece and how the structure displays ideas in a logical manner. Discuss the style and how it augments the piece. Point out the use of consistent tenses and point of view. Examine how the author varied her sentences, used active constructions, relied on strong verbs, and achieved a smooth flow of ideas through effective transitions.

Good writing is almost always a result of good revision. Emphasize that revision is an author's opportunity to make his writing as clear and interesting as possible for his readers. This is the time to put ideas into their final shape.

Revision Peer Consultants

One of the most maddening aspects of revision for students is writing that is not wrong but that could be improved. I once had a student ask me, "How do you know when to stop revising?" This was an excellent question, for which the only answer is, "When you are convinced the material is as strong and clear as you can make it." This, of course, is not the answer students want. Most prefer a simple explanation that tells them when revision is done.

Because they are not sure what they should revise, many students find revision to be a hard part of the writing process. It is difficult for them to step back far enough from their writing to be objective and see the weaknesses in their material.

Sometimes consulting with a partner can help. Partners can read each other's work and offer suggestions for revision. The partners do not correct the papers. Instead, they underline items they feel should be revised and write comments in the margins. The author can then consider the places his partner identified for revision.

When you organize your students into consulting partners, try to pair students who will work well together. For example, best friends, who might have too many things to talk about other than writing, usually do not make a good combination. Another combination you should avoid is that of two students who are easily distracted. Yet another example of a potentially troublesome pair is a student with low self-esteem and a student with a strong personality, who might convince her tentative partner of the need to revise the entire paper even if it requires only minor rewriting.

Ideally, partners should have a separate space in which to work when consulting about writing. While a table in the back of the room is an excellent spot for consulting, in most classrooms pushing desks together is the norm. This arrangement will be satisfactory if students work together quietly and efficiently.

When students are consulting, you should circulate around the room. Observe students, sit in on pairs as necessary, model appropriate behavior, and offer suggestions for revision. However, be careful not to do the revising for your students. The more practice students have with revision, the more comfortable and confident they will become with the process.

Exercise 3.3 Revision Consultants

Divide your students into pairs. If you have an odd number of students in class, you may allow a team of three. Explain that partners are to act as revision consultants. Partners are to read each other's writing and identify instances where they feel revision could improve the piece. Instruct your students to underline where revision might be necessary on their partners' papers. Note that they should write brief comments in the adjacent margins. For example, a spot where a stronger verb could be used ("screamed" instead of "cried out hysterically") might be identified and labeled "Use stronger verb." Remind students that the consultant should not make the revision; this work should be left to the author. After the partner (acting as a consultant) has written and offered comments on the piece, the two students discuss the piece. The consultant explains why he thinks specific instances should be revised.

The writer then either agrees or disagrees. If she agrees that revision is necessary, she may offer possibilities for revising the material and seek the input of her partner. She would then go on to revise the material. If she disagrees, she should offer a reason why she feels revision in this instance is unwarranted.

Learning how to revise efficiently and effectively takes a long time and requires a major effort from you and your students. These efforts are well worth undertaking because revision provides the opportunity to create quality material. It is through revision that your students will truly emerge as writers.

Reproducible Worksheets

Revision is a difficult activity for most students. The worksheets included in this section are designed to provide your students with practice in revision.

The worksheets, which include both articles and stories, cover a variety of topics. Students will find the worksheets challenging in that much of the material that should be revised is not technically wrong, but definitely could be improved. The exceptions are run-on sentences, fragments, unnecessary shifts in tense, faulty point of view, and errors in subject–verb agreement. You should mention to your students that punctuation and capitalization are correct on these worksheets. (Mechanics are addressed in Part 4, "Proofreading.")

The "Guidelines for Revision" handout on page 161 offers students direction for revising their writing. You may find it helpful to distribute copies of the guidelines to your students or to create a poster of the guidelines and display it in your classroom.

Depending on the abilities of your students, you may find it beneficial to work together as a class and revise a few of the worksheets. Such practice can provide students with an excellent model of the revision process. Select examples that you feel would be most helpful to your students. Read through the piece and ask your students for suggestions for revision. Discuss their suggestions. It is probable that students will suggest different ways to revise the same material. Explain that most articles and stories can be revised in various manners, depending on the material and purpose as well as the background and outlook of the writer.

The worksheets proceed from relatively basic to more challenging. The directions for Worksheets 3.1 through 3.13 focus the attention of your students on specific elements to revise, while Worksheets 3.14 through 3.25 simply instruct students to revise the material and do not provide any hints of what weaknesses to look for. Each worksheet has several items that could be revised.

Before assigning any worksheet, review it to make sure it is appropriate for your students. If necessary, go over the instructions and briefly discuss the topic to make sure students understand the material. The focus of students should be on revision, not the material.

Since revised articles and stories will vary, you should accept any reasonable revisions. The Answer Key (page 219) offers a possible revision of each worksheet. After your students have finished their revisions, discuss the revised piece with the class. When students see other ways writing can be revised, their overall understanding of the revision process is enhanced.

Encourage your students to use their developing revision skills in their writing. It is through revision that they will achieve their best writing.

Guidelines for Revision

Asking yourself the following questions can help you revise your writing.

1. Is my topic focused?

2. Is my writing unified? Do all of my ideas and details relate to my topic?

3. Is my organization logical and clear? Does my writing have an opening, body, and closing?

4. Does each paragraph have a main idea? Have I supported each main idea with details and examples?

5. Does my writing style fit my topic?

6. Have I varied my sentence construction?

7. Have I used active rather than passive constructions?

8. Have I used strong verbs?

9. Do my subjects and verbs agree?

10. Did I show and not tell?

11. Are my tenses consistent?

12. Is my point of view consistent?

13. Does my writing flow smoothly? Have I used effective transitions?

14. Have I deleted all unnecessary information and words?

15. Have I said what I want to say and expressed my ideas clearly?

Revision

3.1 Hot Springs and Geysers

A hot spring is water that flows out of the ground at temperatures higher than the air temperature. Most hot springs result from underground water flowing over molten or very hot rock. The rock heats the water. Sometimes the molten rock, which is very extremely hot, can heat the water to such high temperatures that the water turns to steam. If the pressure increases enough, steam and water are pushed toward the surface with great force. The steam and water may spout high into the air. This eruption of steam and water is called a geyser. Most geysers are found in three parts of the world. These three parts of the world are the western United States, Iceland, and New Zealand. The most famous geyser in the world is Old Faithful in Yellowstone National Park. Most geysers erupt at irregular intervals. But this geyser, Old Faithful, erupts on average once every ninety-four minutes each day. Several thousand gallons of hot water shoot up to 170 feet in the air. Watching a geyser is a thrilling experience. It is very exciting to watch a geyser erupt. Geysers are one of nature's most exciting spectacles.

Revision

3.2 Comets

Comets may be thought of as being big, dirty snowballs in space. Scientists believe that most comets are made up of about 75 percent ice and 25 percent dust and rock. When a comet approaches the sun, the heat from the sun causes some of the ice to vaporize. It glows then. As the comet gets closer to the sun, radiation, called the solar wind, sweeps the vaporizing gases away from the comet. The sun is an average star. This produces a tail. Because of the solar wind, which is really radiation, the tail of a comet always streaks away from the sun. No one knows for certain how comets originated. But many scientists believe comets are leftover matter from the time our solar system formed. They do not know how many comets are in our solar system. While most comets remain very, very far from Earth, some have hit our planet. A comet impact is thought to have caused a great explosion in Siberia in 1908. Fortunately, comet impacts are rare. In the past, people looked at comets as evil omens. They thought that comets brought wars, plagues, and death. Today people look at comets with interest and curiosity. They know that comets are just simply dirty snowballs in our solar system.

Revision

3.3 Early History of the Roller Coaster

Directions: Revise the article and make any changes you feel will improve it. Be sure it has an opening, body, and closing. Organize the article into paragraphs and eliminate any unnecessary information. Rewrite the revised article on a separate sheet of paper.

The origin of the modern roller coaster can be traced to Russian ice slides of the seventeenth century. The slides were first built in the mid-1600s in the area around present-day St. Petersburg. St. Petersburg is an important Russian city. The ice slides were large wooden structures. Some were between seventy and eighty feet high. During the winters the slides were enjoyed by a lot of people, including royalty. The slides were covered with ice several inches thick. Large sleds sped down a steep drop that extended hundreds of feet. Stairs were constructed at the backs of the slides for riders to walk up to the top. Some historians believe the Russians also built the first true roller coaster. This first real coaster was a carriage with wheels that ran along a track. There is little evidence. But supposedly it was built in St. Petersburg. This was in the late 1700s. Other historians, however, believe the French built the first coasters with wheels in the early 1800s. Records indicate that two coasters with wheels that locked onto tracks were operating in France around 1817. From these simple and basic designs, the great roller coasters of today have evolved and have become a reality. Roller coaster fans can only wonder what thrills the coasters of tomorrow will provide.

Revision

3.4 Louis Pasteur and the Vaccine for Rabies

Directions: Revise the article and make any changes you feel will improve it. Especially pay attention to logical development. Eliminate any unnecessary information or words. Rewrite the revised article on a separate sheet of paper.

Louis Pasteur (1822–1895) was a great French scientist. One of his many important discoveries was a vaccine for rabies. Pasteur also helped to prove that germs cause disease.

Rabies is an awful, frightening, terrible infection of the nervous system. To become infected, a person or animal must be bitten by an animal that already has the disease. The disease can infect all warm-blooded animals. Before Pasteur's vaccine, the terrible disease called rabies almost always was fatal. It is caused by a virus.

One day a mother brought her nine-year-old son to Pasteur's laboratory. This was in 1885, and Pasteur was working on a vaccine for rabies. Without the vaccine the boy would surely die, because the boy had been bitten by a rabid dog. But the vaccine had not been tested yet on humans. No one knew if it would work. Pasteur agreed to try his vaccine. The boy survived and stayed healthy. The vaccine was successful. A vaccine for rabies had been found.

Since then, thousands of people have been saved from rabies by Pasteur's vaccine. Today, dogs and cats are immunized to prevent them from getting the disease and infecting people.

Revision

3.5 Benefits of Regular Exercise

Directions: Revise the article and make any changes you feel will improve it. Especially pay attention to varying sentence structure and subject–verb agreement. Rewrite the revised article on a separate sheet of paper.

A plan of regular exercise is vital for good health. Regular exercise cause you to breathe more deeply. It makes your heart pump more vigorously. It makes your muscles work harder. It makes your body use more calories. It helps to keep your body at a healthy weight.

Exercising as little as thirty minutes a day can keep your body fit. You should exercise four or five times per week. Regular exercise can also help you think better. It can help you sleep better. It can help you feel better. It benefits your entire body.

You can exercise in various ways. You can walk. You can jog. You can play sports. You can work out in a gym. You can ride your bike. You can skate. You can swim. You can dance. Any activity that make your heart beat faster for a sustained length of time is beneficial.

Exercise is necessary for your health. You should design a practical exercise plan that fit in with your daily schedule.

Revision

3.6 Whale Shark

Directions: Revise the article and make any changes you feel will improve it. Especially pay attention to unity, sentence structure, and subject–verb agreement. Eliminate any unnecessary information. Rewrite the revised article on a separate sheet of paper.

Despite its name, the whale shark is not related to whales at all. Whales are mammals, and sharks are fish. The whale shark are the largest known fish. It may grow to a length of fifty feet. And weigh more than twenty tons. This account for the "whale" part of its name.

Whale sharks are not related to dolphins, either. Dolphins, which are relatives of whales, are mammals.

Whale sharks are found in tropical waters. Around the world. Most of the time they remain in the open sea. They are sighted sometimes near the shore. They are usually solitary creatures. Sometimes they are sighted in schools of dozens or hundreds of individuals.

Whale sharks are known as filter-feeding fish. When feeding, a whale shark swims with its enormous mouth open, sea water flows into its mouth. The water filters through its gills. Small fish, shrimp, and plankton (microscopic plants and animals) are caught.

Unlike many sharks. Whale sharks are not a threat to humans. In fact, divers who study them may approach them without fear. Some divers have actually ridden whale sharks. The sharks does not seem to mind.

Revision

3.7 Destruction of Pompeii

Directions: Revise the article and make any changes you feel will improve it. Especially pay attention to logical development and sentence structure. Eliminate any unnecessary information. Rewrite the revised article on a separate sheet of paper.

Pompeii was a Roman city in ancient Italy. The city was built a few miles south of Mt. Vesuvius. Mt. Vesuvius was an active volcano then. It remains active today. Pompeii was a wealthy city. Pompeii was always busy with commerce and trade.

The day of August 24 in the year A.D. 79, nearly two thousand years ago, began like any other. Without warning. The summit of Vesuvius exploded. Great clouds of smoke and ash were sent high into the sky. Soon the light of the sun was blocked. A terrifying shadow descended over the land.

People awoke that day. They went to work. Began their chores. In the distance Vesuvius sent lazy swirls of dark smoke into the sky, this was normal. No one was worried. The day seemed like any other. There was no cause for worry.

The eruption continued throughout the day and night. Ash bombarded the city. Molten rock bombarded the city. Choking smoke and gas made it impossible to breathe. People panicked. They tried to flee, the streets became jammed, they could not get away in time.

Complete was the destruction of the city. It is estimated that two thousand people died. The doomed city of Pompeii disappeared in a day.

Revision

3.8 Trail to the West

Directions: Revise the article and make any changes you feel will improve it. Especially pay attention to sentence structure and active constructions. Rewrite the revised article on a separate sheet of paper.

The Oregon Trail was the most important pioneer route to the American Northwest. The Oregon Trail was about two thousand miles long. Stretching across the plains and through the mountains. Starting in Independence, Missouri. It ended at the Columbia River in Oregon.

The journey over the trail was long by wagon train. It was difficult, too, and dangerous, the trip could take as long as six months. Most wagon trains managed to travel only about fifteen miles per day.

Many hardships were faced by the pioneers. They had to survive terrible storms, the threat of starvation, and possible attacks by Native Americans. Disease could strike suddenly. It could kill entire families. Sometimes as many as half or more of the people of a wagon train died before reaching Oregon.

Despite the hardships and the heartache. The trail was traveled by thousands of pioneers. They believed that by following the Oregon Trail they would be led to a new life.

Revision

3.9 J. K. Rowling and Harry Potter

Directions: Revise the article and make any changes you feel will improve it. Especially pay attention to sentence structure and active constructions. Rewrite the revised article on a separate sheet of paper.

Joanne Kathleen Rowling was born on July 31, 1965, near Bristol, England. She is known throughout the world as the author of the Harry Potter books.

The idea of writing a fantasy about a young wizard, Harry Potter, was thought of by Rowling in 1990. While she was riding a train. For the next several years the first book of the series was worked on by Rowling.

When she finished the book, Rowling sent it to publishers. The book was turned down by several. Eventually, in 1998, *Harry Potter and the Sorcerer's Stone* was published in the United States. The fantasy focuses on Harry Potter. He is a lonely orphan. He learns that he is a wizard. When Harry enrolls in Hogwarts School of Witchcraft and Wizardry. The magical adventure begins.

The Harry Potter books have proven to be immensely popular, hundreds of millions of the books have been sold. The books have been translated into more than sixty languages and can be bought in two hundred countries, movie versions of the books have been equally popular. Fans around the world continue to be enchanted by the magic of Harry Potter.

Revision

3.10 New House

Directions: Revise the story and make any changes you feel will improve it. Especially pay attention to strong verbs, verb tenses, and distinct descriptions. Rewrite the revised story on a separate sheet of paper.

Vanessa was in her new room in her family's new house. Boxes are everywhere. In some places they were on top of each other right up to the ceiling. The room was enormous, much bigger than her room in the old house. Her old room was little compared to this room. But the new room did not feel like home.

Vanessa sighed. She missed her old house. She misses her old friends. She is worried about making new friends.

After she unpacks a few boxes, Vanessa went downstairs and went outside. She sits on the front steps. She looked around the big yard. There was a rose garden, flower beds, and trees. Vanessa had to admit that the yard was pretty. But she doubted she would ever feel at home here.

A little while later, Vanessa noticed a girl at the house across the street. The girl started coming toward her. The girl is about her own age.

"Hi, I'm Rebecca," the girl says. She had a friendly smile. "But my friends call me Becky. . . ."

Revision

3.11 Room Disaster

Directions: Revise the story and make any changes you feel will improve it. Especially pay attention to varying sentence structure and distinct descriptions. Rewrite the revised story on a separate sheet of paper.

Marcus was in his room. He could not find his history report. He looked around the room. He thought of how messy it was. No, he decided. It was more than messy. It was a disaster.

He tried to remember where he had put the report. He had finished it yesterday. He finished it after school. Then he had played games online with his friends.

He looked at his desk. So much stuff was on it that he could hardly see the top. He searched through the things on it. He searched the drawers. He searched through the things that lay on his dresser. He searched under his bed. All he found there were old sneakers.

Where was the report? He was desperate. Suddenly he remembered.

He picked up his knapsack. He had put the report in the knapsack yesterday so that he would not lose it. He looked inside. There it was.

Marcus heard the school bus. The driver honked the horn. Marcus grabbed his knapsack. He went to the door. The school bus was driving away.

3.12 The Rocket

Directions: Revise the story and make any changes you feel will improve it. Especially pay attention to strong verbs and verb tenses. Rewrite the revised story on a separate sheet of paper.

Gabriela was in front of the big roller coaster. Anthony, her younger brother, was with her.

The roller coaster was called the Rocket. It was the biggest and fastest coaster Gabriela had ever seen. She had been looking forward to riding it for weeks. But now she is not sure she wants to. Gabriela likes fast rides, but this one makes her scared.

"Come on, Gabriela," says Anthony. "Let's get in line." He takes her hand and started pulling her toward the line of people waiting to ride the Rocket.

At first Gabriela does not move. It was as if her feet will not go. She looks at the coaster as it goes slowly to the top of the tracks. Reaching the peak, it comes roaring down so fast that Gabriela was certain she felt the ground shake.

"Gabriela, come on," said Anthony. "You're not afraid, are you?"

Gabriela gave him a smile. If her little brother was not afraid, she should not be afraid either. She takes a deep breath.

"Let's go," Gabriela says. She led Anthony to the line.

Revision

3.13 Pressure Shot

Ten seconds were left in the championship soccer game between the Lions and the Falcons. The score was tied 2 to 2.

Kara Johnson, the Lions' youngest player, was dribbling the ball upfield toward the Falcons' goal. Her heart was going fast. She was tense. Kara was only in the game because Sharon Wilson, the Lions' best scorer, had been hurt earlier.

As Kara went by a Falcon defender, she saw a small opening toward the right side of the field. I tried to keep all of my attention focused on the ball. I knew I would have only one chance for a shot.

She went by another defender and kept moving.

"Take the shot, Kara!" I heard Sharon's voice from the sideline above the noise of the crowd.

Kara looked at the goal. The goalie was in position, staring at me. I knew I could not shoot the ball past her like this.

Kara tried to trick the goalie into thinking she was about to try a shot. She moved to her left to gain a better angle. She kicked the ball as hard as she could.

The goalie could not stop the ball, and I watched the ball go into the goal.

Revision

Name _____ Date _____

3.14 Stars

On a clear night a person can see a few thousand stars. You must be away from the lights of cities and towns to see this many stars. This is only a tiny part of a universe that contains billions of galaxies. Each galaxy contain billions of stars. Stars are giant balls of burning gases. They are made up mostly of hydrogen. This is a gas. Inside a star enormous pressure results in nuclear fusion. During fusion, hydrogen atoms are fused. Or forced together, to make helium. During fusion great amounts of energy is produced. The heat and light of a star are created by fusion. The closest star to the Earth is the sun. Without the light and heat of the sun, the Earth would be a cold, dark, lifeless planet. In recent years, it has been discovered by astronomers that numerous stars have planets orbiting them. Our solar system no longer appears to be unique. In fact, it may be quite ordinary. Although we do not yet have the technological capability to travel to distant stars. Maybe someday we will. How wondrous it will be to find Earth-like planets in orbit around other stars. Future generations of human beings would in time makes their homes throughout the stars.

Revision

3.15 About Bears

Bears are large mammals. They have heavy bodies, short tails, and rounded ears. Although they are classified as carnivores. Most bears also eat grasses, herbs, berries, nuts, and honey. Carnivores are meat-eaters. There are several kinds of bears. North American black bears, grizzly bears, and polar bears are among the most well known. North American black bears are native to North America. This is as their name implies. Black bears are one of the smallest bears. They weigh between two hundred and four hundred pounds. Grizzly bears are much larger than black bears. They can weigh up to a thousand pounds. Grizzlies may be brown, black, or cream-colored. The fur on their shoulders and backs are often tipped with white. This gives them a "grizzled" look. Polar bears are some of the biggest bears. They may be ten feet tall and weigh up to fifteen hundred pounds. They live on the islands of the Arctic Ocean. Seals, young walruses, and fish are hunted by polar bears. In the past, bears are found throughout much of the world. Today they are found mostly in wilderness areas.

3.16 New Madrid, Missouri, Earthquake

Directions: Revise the article and make any changes you feel will improve it. Rewrite the revised article on a separate sheet of paper.

On December 16, 1811, the residents of New Madrid, Missouri, were awakened by a powerful earthquake. This was the first of three great earthquakes. And thousands of lesser aftershocks that struck the region during the winter of 1811–1812.

Many scientists are convinced that the New Madrid earthquakes were among the most powerful ever experienced in North America. If such quakes occurred today in the region. The destruction would be unimaginable. The quakes were so strong that tremors were felt from Canada to Mexico and from the Rocky Mountains to the East Coast. So strong were the quakes that several towns in the region were destroyed, islands in the Mississippi River disappeared, and new lakes were formed. Eyewitness accounts of survivors reported wide cracks opening in the ground, the ground rolling in waves, and large sections of land rising and sinking, damage from the quakes was reported as far away as Charleston, South Carolina, and Washington, DC.

When the next great earthquake will strike the region cannot be predicted by scientists. Many worry that another major quake is only a matter of time.

Revision

3.17 Dr. Daniel Hale Williams

Directions: Revise the article and make any changes you feel will improve it. Rewrite the revised article on a separate sheet of paper.

Daniel Hale Williams (1858–1931) is an African-American physician. He performed the first successful heart surgery. This happened in 1893.

On July 9th of that year, James Cornish, a young man, was stabbed in the chest. He was brought to Provident Hospital. Williams was a surgeon there. Cornish has lost much blood. He needed surgery to stop the bleeding. In those days internal operations almost always result in death from infection. Williams knew that. Without surgery Cornish would surely die. Williams decided to operate.

During surgery, Williams found that Cornish's pericardium had been wounded. The pericardium is a sac of tissue that surrounds the heart. Williams washed the wound with a salt solution. He was hoping this would reduce the chance for infection. He stitched the wound, then he completed the operation. James Cornish survived. He lived for many more years afterward.

Williams goes on to become one of the most respected surgeons of his day. He became, in 1913, the first African-American to be inducted into the American College of Surgeons.

Revision

3.18 Ice Skater

With incredibly and extremely nervous fingers Caitlyn laced her ice skates. She took a deep breath. Hoping to steady the uneasiness in her stomach.

"Don't worry," her coach said. "This time you'll do it."

That only made Caitlyn worry more. Caitlyn recalled her first attempt at completing an axel. A jump with one and a half turns in the air. She had jumped. But had fallen on her landing. The sharp, knifing pain of her breaking ankle would forever be remembered by Caitlyn. Months passed before her ankle was fully healed.

It was only a few weeks ago that Caitlyn had started skating again. She had not attempted an axel, she would today.

Caitlyn stood, stepped onto the ice, and began skating, her heart was thumping.

"You can do it," she was told by her coach.

Caitlyn nodded, forced a weak smile.

She skated around the rink. Trying to build up her courage.

Gaining speed, she knew it was now or never. She pushed off the ice and propelled herself into the air. She spun.

Her landing was good enough to be perfect.

Revision

3.19 Arctic Tern

Arctic terns are small seabirds. They are champion travelers. They make the longest migration of any bird.

Each year Arctic terns fly from the Arctic to Antarctica. Then they fly back to the Arctic. The total distance is nearly twenty-two thousand miles. This is approximately the circumference of the Earth. You have probably learned about circumference in your math class, when studying geometry.

The terns spend the northern summers in the Arctic tundra. They breed there and make their nests. The northern winter approaches, the terns begin flying southward. They finally reach the edge of the Antarctic ice pack. The seasons of the northern and southern hemispheres are reversed. It is now summer in Antarctica. Once summer in Antarctica ends, the terns begin flying northward again. They return to the Arctic.

Arctic terns are only twelve to fifteen inches long and weigh less than a pound. They are well adapted for their long journeys. They have strong wings and streamlined bodies. They eat small fish, shrimp, and krill. Terns swoop down into the water to catch their prey.

Arctic terns have a life span of about twenty years, they spend much of their lives flying.

Revision

3.20 Ancient Olympics

Directions: Revise the article and make any changes you feel will improve it. Rewrite the revised article on a separate sheet of paper.

The ancient Olympic Games were played in Greece. They were played in the wooded valley of Olympia. The ancient games were held for over a thousand years. They were held every four years. They were begun in 776 B.C. and continued until A.D. 393. This is a long time by anyone's standards.

No one knows who organized the first games. According to myth, Hercules started the games. Hercules was a legendary hero known throughout Greece. The poet Pindar, in a poem he wrote in the fifth century B.C., claims a warrior named Pelops created the games. This was in celebration of a great victory.

The first Olympics were rather small. Only one event was held. This was the stade. It was a footrace of about two hundred yards. In time, a forty-thousand-seat stadium was built, more races were added, as well as wrestling, chariot racing, and the pentathlon were added. The pentathlon was a five-part event that included running, wrestling, jumping, and throwing the discus and javelin. People from all over Greece came to watch the games.

The Olympics were enormously popular. In times of war, truces were called. This allowed athletes and spectators to travel to Olympia safely. It is upon this grand tradition that the modern Olympic Games are founded.

Revision

3.21 Dinosaurs and Birds

When you see a bird. You are looking at a descendant of a dinosaur. Many scientists are now convinced that birds are directly related to the dinosaurs. That walked the Earth millions of years ago.

The evidence for the dinosaur–bird link is strong. Just like modern birds, many dinosaurs walked on their hind legs. They had three forward-pointing toes. They also had long tails. In the 1990s, paleontologists found fossils of dinosaurs in northeastern China. Many of these fossils all had evidence of feathers. Not long after this time, more fossilized skeletons of dinosaurs were found. They showed evidence of feathers and other birdlike features.

The best evidence came in 2000. The fossil of a small dinosaur was found by paleontologists. They named this dinosaur *Microraptor zhaoianus*. It was about the size of a crow. This fossil closely resembled a bird.

Despite the evidence of birdlike features. Most scientists do not consider these dinosaurs to be true birds. At least not what we think of as being birds. It is much, much more likely these creatures are a link between dinosaurs and birds.

The dinosaurs are extinct. Their descendants are alive and well.

Revision

3.22 The Maya

Directions: Revise the article and make any changes you feel will improve it. Rewrite the revised article on a separate sheet of paper.

The Maya were among the most advanced native civilizations of the Americas. Starting around 2600 B.C. They slowly gained power and influence. The Maya came to control much land. Today much of this land is now southern Mexico, Guatemala, Belize, and Honduras.

From about A.D. 200 through 900, their society was among the most advanced in the world. The Maya constructed great cities. They constructed magnificent buildings. They constructed pyramids that served as temples. They developed hieroglyphic writing. They developed an accurate calendar. Mayan astronomers recorded the movements of the sun, planets, and stars.

Around 900, the Maya started to decline. No one knows why. Some historians believe the decline might have been caused by several factors. Including wars, disease, and crop failures over a period of years. This much is known. Cities in southern areas were abandoned. The cities of the north were overcome by an invading group known as the Toltecs.

The Spanish arrived in the sixteenth century. Only a few Mayan cities remained. The great civilization was gone.

Revision

3.23 Never Enough Time

Directions: Revise the story and make any changes you feel will improve it. Rewrite the revised story on a separate sheet of paper.

On Saturday morning Darien woke up very early, much earlier than he usually did. He had so very much to do.

After a quick breakfast of cereal, milk, and juice, Darien rode his bike to soccer practice. He was the goalie for his team, he liked soccer, he had been playing soccer since first grade. He likes to play other sports too.

After lunch, Darien helped his father with work around the house. They planted five new shrubs on the side of the house. His father then waters the shrubs. At the same time, Darien weeds the flower beds. They finished the yard work. They cleaned the garage. This took the rest of the afternoon.

After dinner, Darien's friends came over. His friends were Peter and Ricky. The boys decided to play video games. They play several games. The evening passed quickly, very quickly.

By the time his friends went home, Darien was exhausted. He went to bed. Darien thought of all the things he had to do tomorrow.

Revision

3.24 Kangaroo

Kangaroos are found in Australia and on nearby islands. Most people are not aware that there are about a hundred different species, or kinds, of kangaroos. These range from the tiny kangaroo rat to the giant kangaroo.

The giant kangaroo is one of the best-known species of kangaroo. It is also called the great gray kangaroo. Giant kangaroos stand about five feet tall. They weigh up to 150 pounds. They have a tail of about four feet long. They have sheeplike heads, big ears, short front legs, and large, powerful, exceedingly strong hind legs. With its powerful legs, a giant kangaroo can jump thirty feet in a single hop. It can reach speeds of up to forty miles per hour.

Kangaroos are marsupials. Female marsupials carry their young in pouches. A female kangaroo carries her young in her pouch. A young kangaroo is called a joey. The mother carries the joey in her pouch until it is old enough to survive on its own.

Kangaroos are timid creatures. When attacked, they can be dangerous. They will use their forepaws to "punch" an attacker. They will also use their hind legs to kick and slash. A large kangaroo can seriously injure a person.

Revision

3.25 Myth of Phaeton

Directions: Revise the story and make any changes you feel will improve it. Rewrite the revised story on a separate sheet of paper.

In ancient Greek mythology, Phaeton was the son of Apollo. He was the god of the sun. One day Phaeton went to his father's beautiful and magnificent palace of the sun. Apollo is so pleased to see his son that he promises to grant Phaeton anything he asked.

Phaeton had one desire. He wants to drive Apollo's chariot of the sun across the sky.

Apollo knew this could not be. He warned his son. That no one else—not even the other gods—could drive the chariot of the sun.

Phaeton would not be swayed from his demand. Apollo reluctantly agrees.

Phaeton climbed into the chariot. He whipped the horses. The mighty animals gallop into the sky. They pull the bright sun behind the chariot. But Phaeton quickly lost control of them. They ran low to the Earth. The blazing, hot sun burned the ground and all on it.

Zeus, king of the gods, realized Earth was being destroyed. He hurls a lightning bolt at Phaeton. The boy was killed. The Earth was saved.

From that day on, all understood. Only Apollo could drive the sun's chariot across the sky. And they knew that a person should not try to seize control of natural forces.

Proofreading

Proofreading is the part of the writing process that puts the final polish on a piece. Proofreading should not be done until writing has been revised. It is a time for authors to catch and correct any remaining errors in punctuation, capitalization, spelling, and word usage that were missed during revision. Proofreading is the final preparation before writing is shared with an audience.

Some students mistakenly believe that proofreading is the easiest of the stages of the writing process. Because revision has been completed, they feel that the writing is done and that proofreading is nothing more than a final glance through the piece to catch any obvious remaining oversights.

Proofreading, however, is just as demanding as the other stages of writing. While it is true that most errors have been corrected by this time, the errors that remain often are subtle ones that can be hard to find. By now the author may have become so close to the piece that mistakes at this point are not apparent. Moreover, the author is anxious to finish the piece, and he may proofread in haste or without the necessary attentiveness. If an author has done a thorough job of revision, proofreading is much like looking for the proverbial needle in a haystack. This makes proofreading particularly challenging for middle school students, who, given the natural energy levels of their age, are anxious to move on to the next activity as quickly as possible.

For just about every piece, no matter how diligent the writer was during revision, a few mistakes remain. Proofreading requires concentration and a good eye.

Proofreading Strategies

Proofreading is different from ordinary reading, which includes a significant amount of skimming. For most material, the average reader focuses on only a few words per line and skims the rest. This is usually enough for the reader to gain an understanding of the material. Proofreading, though, requires that the proofreader read and examine every word and punctuation mark.

When done properly, proofreading is slow, tedious work. Anything less is likely to be inadequate.

Exercise 4.1 A Proofreading Plan

Explain to your students that every writer must proofread her work to correct any remaining mistakes before she can say it is finished. Proofreading is the last step before sharing writing with readers. Write these general guidelines on an overhead projector or the board and discuss them with your students:

1. Read slowly and concentrate on punctuation, capitalization, spelling, and word usage.
2. Look at the page to make sure paragraphs are fully indented, margins are correct, and there are no gaps in spacing.
3. Proofread the piece two or three times. It is likely that each time a few more minor errors will be found. Only when no more errors are found is proofreading done.

Instruct your students to select an example of their work to proofread. This might be a previously completed piece, or a piece that they have just finished. Have them proofread the piece with care and concentration.

Encourage your students to follow these suggestions whenever proofreading their work. With practice and experience, every writer eventually develops her own methods for proofreading.

Proofreading and Computer Screens

Without doubt, computers have made the work of most writers easier. The capabilities of the machines for composing and revising are without question. Proofreading on a computer screen, however, poses problems for many writers.

Reading text on a computer screen can be trying to the eyes. Consequently, some writers tend to read material with less deliberation than they do with text printed on paper. In addition, text on paper has a different "look" than text on a screen, even in a print preview. When an author reads text on paper, he is more apt to concentrate and examine words and punctuation with greater care.

Of course, some writers do quite well proofing on a computer screen, and I suspect that many of the current generation of students will eventually fall into this category. Growing up with computers and playing countless video games will provide them with a high level of comfort writing, revising, and proofreading written material on a computer screen.

Exercise 4.2 Proofreading on the Screen

Because it is likely that many of your students will do at least some of their proofreading on a computer, you should present the following guidelines on an overhead projector or the board:

1. Read slowly and carefully. [Explain that most people tend to read faster on a computer screen than a printed page.]
2. Use the cursor to go through text one line at a time.
3. Read every word of each line before going to the next line.
4. Concentrate on every piece of punctuation.
5. Use the print preview to check the page for paragraphs, skipped spaces, and unnecessary returns.

After discussing the guidelines, encourage your students to proofread a finished piece on a computer screen. Suggest to them that if they are not comfortable proofing on a computer screen, they should print the material and proof the printed text.

Grammar and Spelling Checkers

These days, just about all word-processing software includes grammar and spelling checkers. Encourage your students to use these helpful programs, but caution them of the limitations such programs have. Grammar checkers may flag sentence structure that is correct but slightly unconventional. Spelling checkers will flag any word that is not in their dictionary. Moreover, in many cases, a spelling checker will offer several alternatives for correction that are not the word the student had in mind. In the cases of both grammar and spelling checkers, students must recognize what is right and what is wrong. When in doubt, encourage your students to consult a grammar book or dictionary, both of which should always be nearby during proofreading.

Proofreading Partners

The work of just about every writer—whether student or professional—benefits from the attention of an editor. Obviously, the more skilled an editor is, the greater the benefits, but in most cases even student editors can help a classmate during proofreading. Because students often have trouble stepping back from their writing to view their work objectively, proofreading can be difficult for them. The author may pass over minor, subtle errors that others quickly recognize. A proofreading partner can help find many of the errors that the writer may overlook.

Proofreading partners should be students who work well together. Sometimes good friends turn out to be ideal partners who help each other, but most of the time friends find it hard to concentrate on work when they are together. You should match students who will complement each other during proofreading.

I encourage students to have a dictionary and grammar book handy when they are proofreading. An author's style book is also helpful. Having such books at hand makes it easier for students to consult them. During proofreading students should underline any errors they find in their partner's work. An alternative to marking clean pages is to use stick-on notes. If partners cannot agree whether an item is wrong, they should consult an appropriate reference book, then check with you only after consulting references.

Exercise 4.3 Partners for Proofing

Organize your students into proofreading pairs. If you have an odd number of students in class, you may allow a team of three. Explain that partners are to proofread each other's writing and identify any remaining errors in punctuation, capitalization, spelling, or word usage. Instruct your students to underline any mistakes they find, or use stick-on notes. After proofreading, the proofreader consults with the author and notes the mistakes she found. If the author disagrees with any of the supposed mistakes, the students check a reference source. The author then corrects any mistakes and proceeds to produce the final copy. I encourage every student to proofread the piece once more and correct any mistakes that may have managed to slip through the previous proofreadings. The students then switch roles; the previous author becomes the proofreader for her partner's work and the previous proofreader assumes the role of author.

Proofreading is not a task of writing to be taken lightly. It is the final preparation of a piece for its audience.

Reproducible Worksheets

Proofreading is a challenging task for most students. The worksheets in this section are designed to provide your students with practice in proofreading.

The worksheets, which include both articles and stories, cover a variety of topics. Errors are concentrated in punctuation, capitalization, and word usage.

The "Guidelines for Proofreading" handout on page 192 offers students direction in their proofreading efforts. You may find it helpful to distribute copies of the guidelines to your students or to create a poster of the guidelines and display it in your classroom.

Depending on the abilities of your students, you may decide to work together as a class and proofread a few of the worksheets. The practice can help students to recognize the types of errors they should look for during proofreading. Choose worksheets that you feel would be most beneficial. Read through the piece as a class, then ask your students to identify the errors. Correct the worksheet together.

The worksheets proceed from relatively basic—for example, focusing on end punctuation, commas, and capitalization—to more challenging. Along with general errors in punctuation and capitalization, the directions for Worksheets 4.1 through 4.15 focus the attention of students on specific errors. Worksheets 4.16 through 4.25 simply instruct students to proofread and do not provide any hints of what to look for. The worksheets average about ten errors each, some a few less and some a few more. Many of the errors are obvious; some are tricky and require sharp concentration.

Before assigning a worksheet, I suggest that you review it to make sure it is appropriate for your students. If necessary, go over the instructions and briefly discuss the topic to make certain that students understand the material. When proofreading, students should not be hampered by unfamiliar or difficult material.

The Answer Key for the worksheets begins on page 219. Note: While most of the corrections are clear-cut, a few, especially concerning the use of commas, are open to interpretation of the context. Accept reasonable corrections in such cases.

After your students have proofread and corrected a worksheet, you should go over the worksheet with the class. This enables students to see any errors that they might have failed to correct.

As students gain experience with proofreading, their proofreading skills will grow. Proofreading will help them to present polished writing to their readers.

Guidelines for Proofreading

Use the following guidelines when proofreading your writing.

1. Sentences begin with capital letters.

2. Sentences end with correct punctuation.

3. Paragraphs are indented.

4. Proper nouns and proper adjectives are capitalized.

5. Commas are used correctly (between the items in a list, to connect compound sentences, and after introductory words, phrases, and clauses).

6. Apostrophes are used correctly (with possessive nouns and contractions).

7. Pronouns are used correctly.

8. Quotation marks are used correctly (for dialogue, and for the titles of short stories, articles, poems, and songs).

9. Italics and underlining are used correctly (for the titles of books, the names of newspapers and magazines, and the titles of CDs, television shows, and movies).

10. Words are used correctly (especially homophones such as *there, their,* and *they're; your* and *you're; its* and *it's; whose* and *who's; hear* and *here; for* and *four; buy, by,* and *bye;* and *to, too,* and *two*).

Proofreading

4.1 Lightning and Thunder

Directions: Proofread and correct the article. Pay close attention to errors in ending punctuation, commas, and capitalization. Make your corrections on this sheet.

If you have ever been caught in a thunderstorm you may have been frightened by the lightning and thunder. Have you ever wondered what causes lightning and thunder.

The air within a thunderstorm is turbulent. As warm air rises and cool air falls water droplets, and ice crystals crash into each other. These collisions cause electrical charges to build up. Positive charges collect in the upper parts of the clouds, and negative charges collect in the lower parts. To balance the negative charges, positive charges also collect near the ground. As this process continues the charges increase in strength. Because unlike charges attract, Electricity may jump from one cloud to another, or between a cloud and the ground. We see this, as lightning.

A lightning bolt is extremely hot. It heats air Molecules and causes them to expand violently This causes a powerful vibration that we hear as thunder.

Thunder can be loud and frightening, but lightning is dangerous. when a thunderstorm approaches you should seek shelter indoors. Stay away from windows, and doors, and do not use electrical equipment. If you are outside, never stand near a tree? Trees can attract lightning. A lightning strike can be fatal.

Proofreading

4.2 Study Tips for Tests

Many students do not know how to study for tests. Are you one of them. If you think you are, the following tips can help.

Preparation for any test, begins long before the day of the test. Keep up with your daily work and take accurate notes On the days leading up to the test, listen to any reviews your teacher gives. This will help you to identify what may be on the test. This in turn, will help you to study the right material. If you have any questions about any of the material, ask your Teacher?

A day, or two before the test, you should go over your notes and key parts of your textbook. Do not wait until the last minute to study. students who study ahead of time, usually do better than those who cram at the last minute.

Get a good night's sleep before the test wake up on time, and eat a solid breakfast. Take the test with confidence. If you have studied effectively you are likely to do well.

4.3 Family Gathering

Directions: Proofread and correct the story. Pay close attention to errors in ending punctuation, commas, and capitalization. Make your corrections on this sheet.

Martina woke up early on thanksgiving morning. Anxious to start the day, she dressed quickly and scampered downstairs

She found her mother in the Kitchen preparing food to take to Martina's grandmother's house. That was where the entire family gathered every thanksgiving for dinner. All of Martina's Uncles Aunts and cousins would be there

After breakfast, Martina helped her mother pack food in a big cooler. They packed, salad, fresh vegetables, fruits, and two cream pies.

Martina's grandmother lived about three hours away, and the drive seemed to take forever. As they drove Martina wondered how many family members had already arrived? When Martina's father pulled into the driveway, she saw several cars.

Martina smiled. Everyone was here. Having Thanksgiving with the family was always, a wonderful time.

Proofreading

4.4 From Tadpole to Frog

Directions: Proofread and correct the article. Pay close attention to errors in ending punctuation, commas, and capitalization. Make your corrections on this sheet.

Frogs are interesting Creatures. They go through metamorphosis, a complete change in structure during their lives They begin life as a fishlike tadpole and grow into a frog.

Tadpoles hatch from eggs. They breathe with gills have streamlined bodies, and have tails. They feed on algae, and tiny Vegetation

As a tadpole matures, its gills disappear lungs develop and legs start to grow. In time the tadpole starts eating insects and larger plant matter.

After about nine weeks of life, the tadpole looks more like a frog with a tail than a tadpole. Eventually the tail is absorbed into the tadpole's body. by about the fourth month of its life, a tadpole has made the transition to a frog. Metamorphosis is finished

The Cycle is now ready to repeat. Female frogs lay their eggs in water, from which a new generation of tadpoles hatches.

4.5 Madam C. J. Walker

Directions: Proofread and correct the article. Pay close attention to errors in ending punctuation, commas, and capitalization. Make your corrections on this sheet.

Madam C. J. Walker, (1867–1919), was the most successful African-American businesswoman of the early twentieth Century. She became the first African-American woman Millionaire.

Madam Walker, whose birth name was Sarah Breedlove built a company that sold hair products for African-American women. To help the company grow; Madam Walker tirelessly promoted her products. By 1910, her company had become so successful that she was able to put others in charge of the day-to-day operations. This allowed her to devote more time to lecture on issues that affected African americans. In her later years, Madam Walker supported numerous African-American schools charities and organizations

When Madam Walker died, at the age of fifty-one, she was thought to be the wealthiest African-American woman in the United States. Her life was an inspiration to women throughout the Country.

Proofreading

4.6 The Key

Directions: Proofread and correct the story. Pay close attention to errors in punctuation and capitalization. Especially pay attention to the use of commas and apostrophes. Make your corrections on this sheet.

Samantha hurried down the empty hallway toward her classroom. School had ended an hour ago and she hoped her classroom was not locked. She needed to get her Science book, which she had forgotten to take home. Without the book, she wouldnt be able to study for the big science test tomorrow.

Science was a difficult subject for Samantha. She had to study more for science than for any other subject.

When she got to her classroom, Samantha was relieved to find the door open. She went inside, expecting to see mrs. Talbot her teacher but the room was empty. Samantha figured that mrs Talbot had gone home for the day.

As Samantha walked by the teachers desk, she noticed a paper on it. Her eyes widened. It was the answer key to the test. The key could help her get a good grade.

Samantha stood there for a long moment. Taking the answers would be cheating and that was wrong.

She went to her desk got her science book, and left the room.

4.7 First Flight

People have dreamed about flying for thousands of years. Early ideas ranged from mechanical wings that could enable a person to fly like a bird; to strange machines with flapping blades. None, of course worked.

As time passed, people looked for other ways to fly. A breakthrough came in france in 1782.

Joseph and Jacques Montgolfier, two Brothers were interested in flying. While sitting by a fireplace, Joseph filled a paper bag with smoke and hot air. As the Brothers watched the bag float up to the ceiling they got an idea.

The Montgolfier's began to experiment. They made balloons out of paper and linen and filled them with hot air from a fire. When they released the balloons the balloons rose. The brothers built bigger and bigger balloons until they built one able to carry people.

Finally, in November of 1783, two people, flew in a Montgolfier balloon. This first flight lasted twenty-five minutes and covered about five miles. The dream of flight became, a reality.

Proofreading

4.8 Shaking Earth

Earthquakes may best be described as a shaking of the Earth. Thousands of earthquakes occur each year but only one out of five is strong enough to be felt. On average, of every thousand earthquakes only two cause damage

Earthquakes are caused by movement of the Earths crust. The Earth's crust, which is it's outer layer is divided into great pieces. These pieces called plates are made of rock. The plates move slowly in different directions. They may grind past each other away from each other or toward each other. Sometimes a long crack, called a fault, forms between plates. The famous San Andreas fault in california is a result of two plates grinding past each other. If enough stress builds up along a fault an earthquake occurs.

Minor earthquakes cause little damage, and few injuries. Major quakes can destroy entire cities and result in thousands of deaths.

Proofreading

4.9 Track Meet

Directions: Proofread and correct the story. Pay close attention to errors in punctuation and capitalization. Especially pay attention to the use of commas, apostrophes, and quotation marks. Make your corrections on this sheet.

It was the biggest regional Track Meet of the season. Andrew stretched and tried to shake the nervous tension, from his body. So far this year he had won all of the two-mile races he had entered but now he was facing boys who might be faster and have greater endurance.

The official called the boys to the starting line. Andrew took a deep breath and stepped forward.

"Remember Andrew," Coach Simmons said, "Pace yourself. Make sure you're strong for the end."

Andrew nodded. He took his position on the inside lane. He thought about his coachs advice. Andrew sometimes made the mistake of running too hard in the first part of a race. When he did that he would fade at the end.

"On your mark! said the official. Get set! Go!"

The race began.

Andrew was in the middle of the pack of runners his strides long and easy. It was a long way to the end of the race. He would make sure he was strong for the finish.

Proofreading

4.10 Business Letter

123 River Drive

Green Valley NJ 00000

Oct 25 2007

Ms Janice Williams, Circulation Manager

Extreme Skateboarding Magazine

50 Reynolds street

Mountain Lake, CA 00000

Dear Ms. Williams,

I would like to subscribe to *Extreme Skateboarding Magazine*. Enclosed is a check for $24.95 for a subscription for one year.

Thank you.

Sincerely Yours'.

Thomas Jackson

Proofreading

4.11 Great Friends

Richie and me are best friends. We've been best friends for about as long as I can remember.

Some kids think its strange that a girl and boy in seventh grade are best friends. But I dont think its strange at all. Richie and me have a lot in common.

We've always lived next door to each other. We both like sports we like the same type of music, and we like the same kinds of Movies. But most important, we just like hanging out together. There's never any trouble between Richie and I. We stick up for each other, and we're always honest with each other. Richies easy to talk to and he's always willing to help when I have a problem. I do the same for him.

No matter what happens I know I can depend on Richie, and he knows he can depend on me. I suppose that, most of all is what makes our friendship so special.

Proofreading

4.12 Amelia Earhart

What happened to Amelia Earhart. People have been trying to answer this question since 1937. That was the year Earhart and Fred J. Noonan her copilot disappeared in their plane near Howland island in the South Pacific.

Amelia Earhart loved to fly. She became famous in may of 1932 when she made a solo flight across the Atlantic ocean. She followed this feat with several solo long-distance flights across the U.S. In January of 1931, she made a solo flight from Hawaii to California.

Earhart attempted her most daring flight in June of 1937. With copilot Noonan, she set off to make an around-the-world flight. On July 2nd there plane vanished. Rescue teams mounted extensive search efforts but no sign of Earhart, Noonan, or they're plane was ever found.

In the following years, researchers and mystery buffs have tried to discover what happened to Amelia Earhart. None have succeeded and Amelia Earharts disappearance remains a mystery.

4.13 Season Opener

Directions: Proofread and correct the story. Pay close attention to errors in punctuation and capitalization. Especially pay attention to quotation marks, apostrophes, and pronouns. Make your corrections on this sheet.

Giorgio stared at the overcast sky. He turned to Danny his friend.

"It looks like rain" Giorgio said.

"According to the weather forecast, said Danny, "theres only a slight chance of showers."

The two boys had just arrived at the baseball field for the first game of the season. Some of the players of both teams were already their.

Coach Bennett instructed the boys to begin warming up.

Giorgio and Danny took their places with there teammates and began playing catch.

Giorgio looked back at the sky. Baseball was his favorite sport and he had been looking forward to this first game for weeks.

Giorgio quit worrying" said Danny. "the game will start on time."

"I hope so," said Giorgio.

A little while later, the sun poked through the clouds.

"See," said Danny. "The suns coming out. Now you'll be worrying about the sun getting into your eyes."

Giorgio smiled. "Your probably right."

Proofreading

4.14 Reading Enjoyment

Directions: Proofread and correct the article. Pay close attention to errors in punctuation and capitalization. Especially pay attention to the use of quotation marks, italics, and apostrophes. Make your corrections on this sheet.

Step into my house, and you will find books and magazines everywhere. Everybody in my family enjoys reading. We read for entertainment, and information.

My father rides the bus to work each morning. During his commute he reads "The New York Times." He also reads magazines. His favorites are *Time* and *Discover.*

My mother enjoys reading novels. She reads a new novel every week. She likes mysteries the best but she also likes romances. Sometimes she likes a book so much that she cant put it down until she finishes it.

Jessica, my older sister likes short stories and poems. One of her favorite short stories' is *The dinner Party* by Mona Gardner. Her favorite poem is Lewis Carroll's "Jabberwocky."

As for me I mostly read novels. My favorites are fantasies with heroes, evil villains, and magic. If I had to pick one favorite, I would choose *"The Hobbit"* by J. R. R Tolkien.

4.15 Big Slope

Emily stuck her ski poles into the snow to steady herself. She stood on the top of the mountain and looked down the slope. Daredevil trail disappeared in the distance.

She felt a gentle pat on her shoulder.

"You can make it down," said Alyssa her big sister.

"Thats not what worries me, said Emily. She forced a smile. "Im worried about how many broken bones I'll have."

"You don't have too do this, Alyssa said."

"Yes, I do" said Emily, who prided herself on her skill at skiing. "This is the only trail on this mountain I've never gone down."

Alyssa smiled. "You'll be fine," she said. "Keep your knees bent and remember to lean into the turns.

Emily nodded. "Hear I go." She pushed off with her poles and started down the trail.

She heard Alyssas voice behind her.

"You can do it."

As Emily leaned into the first turn she hoped her sister was right.

Proofreading

4.16 Sound Waves

The sounds of laughter, the honking of a car horn and the roar of a lawn mowers motor are all produced in the same way. But do you know how those sounds are produced.

All sounds are a result of vibrations. When something vibrates it moves back and forth rapidly. Imagine plucking a string on a Violin. As the string vibrates, it makes a sound. Of course you seldom see the vibrations that cause sound, because the vibrations are to small and are moving too fast. Unlike plucking a string, imagine tapping a pencil on a desk. You cant see the vibrations but you hear the sound of the tapping.

When an object vibrates it causes the nearby molecules in the air to move. As the molecules move, the vibrations travel through the air in the form of waves. Like the ripples that result from a stone tossed in a pond, the waves move outward from the point of the sound in every direction. When these waves reach your ear, you here the sound.

As sound waves move outward from a vibrating object, they become weaker. This is why a sound becomes fainter the farther away you are from it's source.

4.17 Chess

Have you ever played chess. If you have you have played a game that has been around for at least fifteen hundred years.

Chess is a game of skill, and strategy played by two players. The game is based on the warfare of the Middle Ages. Each player has sixteen pieces that he plays on a square board. The board is divided into sixty-four alternate light and dark squares. When a player lands a peace on a space occupied by one of his opponents pieces, that piece is removed from the board. The object of the game is to capture, or checkmate, the opponent's king. Capture of the king ends the game.

No one knows whom invented chess? Most historians believe the game originated in india about the sixth century A.D. The game slowly spread westward threw Persia (modern Iran) and reached Europe sometime between 700 and 900.

The modern game began to evolve during the sixteenth and seventeenth Centuries. Today, chess is played around the world and is as popular as ever.

Proofreading

4.18 Volcanoes

A volcano is a mountain with a vent, or opening to the interior of the Earth. Magma (hot, melted rock) from inside the Earth passes through the vent to the surface. Sometimes the magma flows out slowly but sometimes it erupts in great explosions.

Volcanoes can be in one of three states, active, dormant, or extinct. An active volcano is erupting or shows signs of erupting soon. A dormant volcano has not erupted in some time but may erupt again in the future. An extinct volcano is no longer capable of erupting.

Volcanic eruptions start far beneath the surface. When magma comes under great pressure, it rises threw cracks and week spots in the rock. Eventually the magma finds it's way to the surface. If the pressure is intense, the magma may erupt. Along with magma, eruptions usually include gases ash, and steam.

Magma that flows out of a volcano is called Lava. Lava can reach temperatures of 2,000 degrees Fahrenheit or more. Flowing down a volcanos sides lava can destroy everything in its path.

Scientists study volcanoes, in the hope of learning how to predict eruptions. Such knowledge would help them warn people before an eruption occurs.

Proofreading

4.19 Looking for Whales

Brianna stepped from the dock and into the boat. She plopped onto the nearest seat. She was not happy being here. Her and her parents were about to spend one of there vacation days in search of whales. Brianna would have preferred to spend the day at the oceanside resort where the family was staying for the weak.

"I've been looking forward to today for months Briannas mother said.

"I haven't." Brianna said. "I'd rather be at the beach."

"You can go to the beach every day for the rest of our vacation said her father. "But if we're lucky, today you can see a whale."

Brianna didnt like boats and she liked the idea of searching for whales even less.

As the boat left the dock, Brianna sighed. This was going to be a long day.

It was early afternoon when the Captain directed everyone to look ahead.

"There! cried one of the passengers.

Brianna looked and saw a magnificent animal rise from the water.

"Its incredible," she said, suddenly glad she was hear and not back on the beach.

Proofreading

4.20 Color the World

One of the most wonderful features of the world is color. Colors help to make things distinct. Just think, of a blue sky, a red rose, or the pure whiteness of freshly fallen snow. Can you imagine how dull the world would be without color.

The basics of colors are surprisingly simple. Colors can be divided into three kinds primary, secondary, and intermediate. The primary colors are red, yellow, and blue. They cant be made bye mixing any other colors. The secondary colors, which are made by mixing to primary colors are orange green, and violet. Mixing red and yellow makes orange. Mixing yellow and blue makes green. Mixing blue and red makes violet. Intermediate colors are made by mixing primary and secondary colors. Mixing white, or black with colors will make them lighter or darker.

Its remarkable that all colors are based on combinations of red, yellow, and blue. The World truly is a colorful place.

Proofreading

4.21 Cat in the Tree

Directions: Proofread and correct the story. Pay close attention to errors in punctuation, capitalization, and word usage. Make your corrections on this sheet.

I was upstairs working on my book report when Marlena my little sister called me from downstairs.

"Come quick Angela!" she cried.

"What's wrong," I said, getting up from my desk and hurrying to the stairs.

"Its Puffin! Marlena said. She's in a big tree. She cant get down." Puffin was our cat.

I hurried downstairs and followed Marlena out the front door.

Looking up at the big oak tree in our yard I saw Puffin sitting on a high branch. She had climbed up but she was afraid to climb down.

"Puffin, come down right now," I said. A mournful meow was my answer.

Their wasn't anything I could do except to keep calling Puffin down. But the cat wouldnt budge.

I was glad when my Father came home from work. He got a ladder, climbed up, and got Puffin.

I smiled as Marlena scolded the foolish cat.

"Puffin I never want you to climb that tree again," she said.

Proofreading

4.22 Catching Rainbows

If you have ever seen a rainbow in the sky you have witnessed one of the beauties of nature. The typical rainbow makes an arc in the sky. Sometimes a rainbow is so big that it's ends seem to touch the Earth.

The mystery of a rainbow lies in sunlight and water droplets. A ray of sunlight contains all the colors of the spectrum, red, orange, yellow, green, blue, and violet. When sunlight shines through water droplets the droplets separate the sunlight into its different colors. Under the right conditions this creates a rainbow.

Rainbows may appear anywhere sunlight shines on water droplets: but they most often are seen near the end of a rain shower. They may also appear in the spray of a waterfall a fountain or a garden hose.

According to Legend a pot of gold awaits you at the end of a rainbow. Of course you can never reach the end. As you approach a rainbow, the rainbow seems to retreat and soon disappears.

Proofreading

4.23 Babysitting Wars

Dawn walked up the steps to the home of Mr. and Mrs Ross and rang the doorbell. This was the first time she was to babysit for Matthew, their son. She hoped Matthew, who was only five years old would behave. Christina, Dawn's best friend babysat for Matthew once, and she vowed never to babysit for him again.

Mrs. Ross opened the door and greeted Dawn with a friendly smile.

Dawn saw Matthew standing in the living room. He was smiling to. He seemed like a nice boy.

After Mrs. Ross gave Dawn instructions, her and her husband got ready to leave.

"Remember Dawn," mrs. Ross said at the door, Matthew must be in bed no later than nine oclock."

"I'll remember." Dawn said.

For the next two hours Dawn read to Matthew, they drew and colored, and they watched Matthews favorite video. Matthew was so pleasant that Dawn began to wonder if Christina had babysat for the same boy.

At nine oclock Dawn told Matthew that it was time for bed.

Matthew looked at her and smiled.

"No!" he said firmly. "And you can't make me go to bed.

Dawn thought of Christina and realized that it was going to be a long night.

Proofreading

4.24 Wrestling Challenge

Directions: Proofread and correct the story. Pay close attention to errors in punctuation, capitalization, and word usage. Make your corrections on this sheet.

It was the final day of wrestling camp. Dan was to wrestle Brett in the championship match for there weight class.

Dan looked at Brett and frowned. He doubted that he could defeat Brett. Brett was a year older and had more experience.

"Bretts a great wrestler," Dan said to Roberto his best friend.

"He is," said Roberto, "But he loses his cool. He likes to pin his opponent's fast. But when that doesn't happen, he gets mad and makes mistakes."

"But how does that help me," said Dan. "He's faster and stronger than I am."

"You have to wrestle smart, said Roberto. "Dont let him gain the advantage. He'll get frustrated and than you make your move."

"You mean stay on defense until he makes a mistake," said Dan.

Roberto nodded.

Soon after the match began, Dan realized his friend was right. When the match was finished Dan was a wrestling champion.

Proofreading

4.25 Deep Space Explorers

Directions: Proofread and correct the story. Pay close attention to errors in punctuation, capitalization, and word usage. Make your corrections on this sheet.

Commander Sarto stood on the bridge of his starship and watched the main viewing screen. As they approached the tiny planet it grew on the screen. Sarto studied the oceans and land masses that appeared through the clouds. The planet reminded him of home.

"Take us into orbit," he said to Jartan his second in command. "Then see if you can listen to they're communications."

Sarto thought of his mission to make contact with the Beings that lived on the planet. He wondered what they were like?

He noticed the concern that had come to Jartans face.

"Whats the matter." Sarto said.

"There must be some mistake," said Jartan. "The transmissions I'm picking up indicate that these beings are quite violent." "Their not ready to join the United Planets."

Sarto sighed. He had seen this happen before.

"Sometimes the first survey teams make errors in there evaluations," Sarto said. "Set course for the next planet. Make a note to visit Earth again in about a hundred years."

Proofreading

Answer Key

Part 1

Answers for the worksheets throughout this section will vary. Accept reasonable answers. Also accept reasonable stories and articles.

Part 2

2.1 Sentences will vary. Accept reasonable sentences.

2.2 Sentences will vary. Accept reasonable sentences.

2.3 Sentences may vary. Possible sentences follow. 1. Carl mowed the lawn and trimmed the hedges. 2. It rained all day, and the soccer game was postponed. 3. Maria and Melinda are twins, but they don't look much like each other. 4. The evening grew darker, and the stars soon appeared. 5. Mandy plays soccer and softball. 6. We might go to a movie, or we might go shopping instead. 7. Juan had to do his history report, but he had to finish his math homework first. 8. The kitten crept up and pounced on the toy mouse.

2.4 Sentences may vary. Possible sentences follow. 2. After LuAnn finished her science assignment, she started her math. 3. Because it snowed heavily all night, the roads were impassable. 4. When the power went off last night, Rob realized he did not have a flashlight. 5. Even though Carla had a sprained ankle, she still went to soccer practice. 6. Once the sky became overcast, the rain began. 7. While Trish was home with a cold, she finished reading *Dicey's Song*. 8. During the middle of the night, strange sounds woke Regina.

2.5 If you sometimes wonder what the difference is between a meteoroid, meteor, and meteorite, you are not alone. Many people find these words confusing. ⌐ Meteoroids are rocky chunks of matter that hurtle through space. While many are the size of a small stone, others may be hundreds of feet wide. Most meteoroids orbit the sun and never approach Earth. Some, however, have orbits that intersect the orbit of the Earth. If these meteoroids come too close, they may be captured by the Earth's gravity and pulled into the Earth's atmosphere. Friction with the molecules in the atmosphere will cause the meteoroid to heat up and disintegrate. ⌐When a meteoroid begins to burn in the atmosphere, it leaves a streak of light. It is now called a meteor, often mistakenly referred to as a shooting star. Although most meteors disintegrate completely before they hit the ground, some make it through the atmosphere and smash into the Earth. ⌐ A meteor that hits the Earth is called a meteorite. If a meteor is big, the impact will result in a great explosion and terrible destruction. ⌐Fortunately, most meteoroids remain far from the Earth. Of those that enter the atmosphere, most disintegrate long before reaching the ground.

2.6 Topic sentences will vary. Possible sentences follow. 1. Leon had a lot of homework. 2. Jon enjoys playing video games. 3. Jenna is very talented. 4. Christy could not find her book report.

2.7 Transitional sentences will vary. Possible sentences follow. 1. She got to the bus stop as the bus was pulling up. 2. Just as he reached his yard, the rain began to pour down. 3. Curious, she took the CD out. 4. Rolling up his sleeves, he got started.

2.8 Details will vary. Possible details follow. 1. Thunder could be heard in the distance. Trees bent in the gusty winds. People were hurrying inside. 2. She put icing on the cake. She finished putting up the final decorations. She made the punch and filled the punch bowl. 3. She read to the twins. They colored. They watched the twins' favorite TV programs. 4. The land was hot and dry. Flowers withered. The grass was brown.

2.9 Sentences will vary. Possible sentences follow. 2. The rain pounded on the roof and ran down the gutters. 3. When rain ruined our picnic, Aunt Loretta smiled and explained how we would have our picnic indoors. 4. Christina looked at her report card and smiled at all the As. 5. The heavy rain caused the rushing river to rise and wash over its banks. 6. Lisa's heart pounded when she heard the noises outside the front door. 7. Martin dribbled past two defenders and shot the ball perfectly through the basket. 8. The storm knocked over trees and damaged the roofs of several houses.

2.10 Some answers may vary. Possible answers follow. 1. piercing (or frightening) 2. deep, invincible 3. blank (or empty) 4. old, frightening (or strange) 5. mighty (or towering) 6. playful (or fluffy), fluffy (or old) 7. outdoor (or physical or exciting) 8. towering (or mighty), cloudless 9. wintry 10. blazing

2.11 Some answers may vary. Possible answers follow. 1. thoroughly (or carefully) 2. always 3. recently (or easily or quickly) 4. intensely 5. completely 6. flawlessly 7. soon 8. quickly 9. easily 10. carefully (or thoroughly)

2.12 Answers will vary. Accept reasonable answers.

2.13 1. Kim was nervous and could not stop fidgeting. This was her first gymnastics competition, and she was afraid she would make mistakes and let her team down. When Carrie, her friend, tried to assure her that she would do fine, Kim smiled. But she still felt nervous. When her coach called her name, Kim stepped forward. She took a deep breath to steady herself and assumed her starting position on the floor.

2. Michael woke up early on Saturday. He knew it was going to be an extremely busy day. That morning, he helped his father mow the lawn and trim the hedges. Right after lunch Michael went to soccer practice. He got home from practice around 4:00 P.M. He watched his younger brother until dinner because his parents had not yet returned from shopping. After dinner Michael did research for his history project. By the time Michael went to sleep that night, he was exhausted.

2.14 2. The wind uprooted the great oak tree. 3. Megan designed the art club's new logo. 4. Trish won the debate. 5. Tony washed the car. 6. Marissa played a violin solo in the eighth-grade winter concert. 7. The fox crept up on the unsuspecting rabbit. 8. The intense snowstorm caused treacherous whiteout conditions. 9. Paula Fox wrote *The Slave Dancer*. 10. Mrs. Carter assigned homework for the spring break.

2.15 Sentences may vary. Possible sentences follow. 2. The hawk soared high over the field in search of prey. 3. The cat crept toward the bird. 4. The girls whispered in the library. 5. Joanna jumped out of the way of the speeding car. 6. The little boy shrieked when he stubbed his toe. 7. Thomas rushed to catch the bus before it pulled away. 8. Alvaro raced to the finish line. 9. The cold winter wind whipped across the open field. 10. The fog blanketed the valley.

2.16 1. present 2. future perfect 3. present 4. past 5. present perfect 6. future 7. past 8. past perfect 9. future 10. present

2.17 1. bakes 2. uses 3. watch 4. jog 5. lives 6. plays 7. helps 8. practice 9. twinkle 10. rises

2.18 I sighed, thinking of all the math and science homework I had to do. I also had to read another chapter in my novel.

I looked at the pile of books on my desk and frowned. I couldn't decide which book to open first, but I knew I had better start if I wanted to meet my friends later.

I opened my math book and began. After I finished ten word problems, I answered my science questions. Finally I read the chapter in my novel.

As soon as I was done, I went to see my friends, who were waiting for me at the basketball court. By the time I arrived, they had already chosen teams. They had saved a spot for me.

2.19 Note: Students may select other names for the third person point of view.

Teresa woke up early on the Saturday of the five-kilometer race. Her father and she would be running to help raise money for charity. She had been jogging with him four times a week for the last several weeks, and she was certain she would finish the race.

Once the race began, though, she wasn't so sure. There were a lot of hills, and they were running into the wind. Teresa began to worry that she would become tired and have to walk to the finish line.

Remembering her father's advice about keeping a slow but steady pace, she kept going. When at last she saw the finish line, she smiled and sprinted the last hundred yards.

Teresa didn't win any trophy. But that was OK. She was satisfied simply having run and finished her first big race.

2.20 Compare: Both elephants have trunks and eat grass and leaves. **Contrast:** African elephants are found mostly in the tropical forests and grasslands of Africa. They are bigger than Indian elephants and can reach a height of thirteen feet. African elephants are tallest at the shoulder, they have larger ears, and their skin is more wrinkled. Both male and female African elephants have tusks. Indian elephants are found in India and Southeast Asia. Indian elephants are tallest at the arch of the back. Only male Indian elephants have tusks.

2.21 Sentences will vary. Accept reasonable sentences.

2.22 1. a passageway or opening 2. knowledge, enlightenment 3. obstacle, hindrance 4. sadness, worry, concern 5. a beginning 6. wisdom 7. a journey 8. infinity, endlessness 9. end, finish 10. slyness

Part 3

Revised articles and stories will vary. Possible revisions are provided.

3.1 A hot spring is water that flows out of the ground at temperatures higher than the air temperature. Most hot springs result from underground water flowing over molten or hot rock.

Sometimes the molten rock can heat the water to such high temperatures that the water turns to steam. If the pressure increases enough, steam and water are pushed toward the surface with great force. The steam and water may spout high into the air. This eruption of steam and water is called a geyser.

Most geysers are found in three parts of the world: the western United States, Iceland, and New Zealand. The most famous geyser in the world is Old Faithful in Yellowstone National Park. Most geysers erupt at irregular intervals, but Old Faithful erupts on average once every ninety-four minutes each day. Several thousand gallons of hot water shoot up to 170 feet in the air.

Watching a geyser erupt is a thrilling experience. Geysers are one of nature's most exciting spectacles.

3.2 Comets may be thought of as being big, dirty snowballs in space. Scientists believe that most comets are made up of about 75 percent ice and 25 percent dust and rock.

When a comet approaches the sun, the heat from the sun causes some of the ice to vaporize and glow. As the comet nears the sun, radiation, called the solar wind, sweeps the vaporizing gases away from the comet. This produces a tail. Because of the solar wind, the tail of a comet always streaks away from the sun.

No one knows for certain how comets originated. But many scientists believe comets are leftover matter from the time our solar system formed. They do not know how many comets are in our solar system.

While most comets remain far from Earth, some have hit our planet. A comet impact is thought to have caused a great explosion in Siberia in 1908. Fortunately, comet impacts are rare.

In the past, people looked at comets as evil omens. They thought that comets brought wars, plagues, and death. Today people look at comets with interest and curiosity. They know that comets are simply dirty snowballs in our solar system.

3.3 The origin of the modern roller coaster can be traced to Russian ice slides of the seventeenth century. The slides were first built in the mid-1600s in the area around present-day St. Petersburg.

The ice slides were large wooden structures, some being between seventy and eighty feet high. The slides were covered with ice several inches thick. Large sleds sped down a steep drop that extended hundreds of feet. Stairs were constructed at the backs of the slides for riders to walk up to the top.

Some historians believe the Russians also built the first true roller coaster. This first real coaster was a carriage with wheels that ran along a track. Although there is little evidence, supposedly it was built in St. Petersburg in the late 1700s.

Other historians, however, believe the French built the first coasters with wheels in the early 1800s. Records indicate that two coasters with wheels that locked onto tracks were operating in France around 1817.

From these basic designs, the great roller coasters of today have evolved. Roller coaster fans can only wonder what thrills the coasters of tomorrow will provide.

3.4 Louis Pasteur (1822–1895) was a great French scientist. One of his many important discoveries was a vaccine for rabies.

Rabies is a terrible infection of the nervous system. It is caused by a virus and can infect all warm-blooded animals. To become infected, a person or animal must be bitten by an animal that already has the disease. Before Pasteur's vaccine, rabies almost always was fatal.

In 1885 Pasteur was working on a vaccine for rabies. One day a mother brought her nine-year-old son to Pasteur's laboratory. The boy had been bitten by a rabid dog, and without the vaccine the boy would surely die. But the vaccine had not been tested yet on humans. Although no one knew if it would work, Pasteur agreed to try his vaccine. The vaccine was successful. The boy survived and stayed healthy.

Since then, Pasteur's vaccine has saved thousands of people from rabies. Today, dogs and cats are immunized to prevent them from getting the disease and infecting people.

3.5 A plan of regular exercise is vital for good health. Regular exercise causes you to breathe more deeply, makes your heart pump more vigorously, and makes your muscles work harder. It makes your body use more calories and helps to keep your body at a healthy weight.

Exercising as little as thirty minutes a day, four or five times per week, can keep your body fit. Regular exercise can also help you think better, sleep better, and feel better. Your entire body benefits from exercise.

You can exercise in various ways. You can walk, jog, or play sports. You can work out in a gym. You can ride your bike, skate, swim, or dance. Any activity that makes your heart beat faster for a sustained length of time is beneficial.

Exercise is necessary for your health. You should design a practical exercise plan that fits in with your daily schedule.

3.6 Despite its name, the whale shark is not related to whales at all. Whales are mammals, and sharks are fish. The whale shark is the largest known fish. It may grow to a length of fifty feet and weigh more than twenty tons. This accounts for the "whale" part of its name.

Whale sharks are found in tropical waters around the world. Most of the time they remain in the open sea, but sometimes they are sighted near the shore. They are usually solitary creatures, but they can also be found in schools of dozens or hundreds of individuals.

Whale sharks are known as filter-feeding fish. When feeding, a whale shark swims with its enormous mouth open. Sea water flows into its mouth and filters through its gills. Small fish, shrimp, and plankton (microscopic plants and animals) are caught.

Unlike many sharks, whale sharks are not a threat to humans. In fact, divers who study them may approach them without fear. Some divers have actually ridden whale sharks. The sharks do not seem to mind.

3.7 Pompeii was a Roman city in ancient Italy, a few miles south of Mt. Vesuvius. Mt. Vesuvius was an active volcano then and remains active today. Pompeii was a wealthy city, busy with commerce and trade.

The day of August 24th in the year A.D. 79 began like any other. People awoke, went to work, and began their chores. In the distance Vesuvius sent lazy swirls of dark smoke into the sky. This was normal and no one was worried.

Without warning the summit of Vesuvius exploded. Great clouds of smoke and ash were sent high into the sky. Soon the light of the sun was blocked, and a terrifying shadow descended over the land.

The eruption continued throughout the day and night. Ash and molten rock bombarded the city. Choking smoke and gas made it impossible to breathe. People panicked and tried to flee, but the streets became jammed. People could not get away in time.

The destruction of the city was complete, and an estimated two thousand people died. The doomed city of Pompeii disappeared in a day.

3.8 The Oregon Trail was the most important pioneer route to the American Northwest. About two thousand miles long, the Oregon Trail stretched across the plains and through the mountains. Starting in Independence, Missouri, it ended at the Columbia River in Oregon.

The journey by wagon train over the trail was long, difficult, and dangerous. Because most wagon trains traveled only about fifteen miles per day, the trip could take as long as six months.

The pioneers faced many hardships. They had to survive terrible storms, the threat of starvation, and possible attacks by Native Americans. Disease could strike suddenly and kill entire families. Sometimes as many as half or more of the people of a wagon train died before reaching Oregon.

Despite the hardships and the heartache, thousands of pioneers traveled the trail. They believed that the Oregon Trail would lead them to a new life.

3.9 Joanne Kathleen Rowling was born on July 31, 1965, near Bristol, England. She is known throughout the world as the author of the Harry Potter books.

Rowling thought of the idea of writing a fantasy about Harry Potter, a young wizard, while she was riding a train in 1990. She worked on the first book of the series for the next several years.

When she finished the book, Rowling sent it to publishers. Several turned the book down. Eventually, in 1998, *Harry Potter and the Sorcerer's Stone* was published in the United States. The fantasy focuses on Harry Potter, a lonely orphan who learns that he is a wizard. When Harry enrolls in Hogwarts School of Witchcraft and Wizardry, the magical adventure begins.

The Harry Potter books have proven to be immensely popular. Hundreds of millions of the books have been sold. The books have been translated into more than sixty languages and can be bought in two hundred countries. Movie versions of the books have been equally popular. The magic of Harry Potter continues to enchant fans around the world.

3.10 Vanessa stood in her new room in her family's new house. Boxes were everywhere. In some places they were piled on top of each other right up to the ceiling.

Vanessa sighed. The room was enormous, much bigger than her room in the old house. But the new room did not feel like home. She missed her old house and her old friends. She was worried about making new friends.

After she unpacked a few boxes, Vanessa walked downstairs and went outside. She sat on the front steps. She looked around the big yard at a beautiful rose garden, colorful flower beds, and tall trees. Vanessa had to admit that the yard was pretty, but she doubted she would ever feel at home here.

A little while later, Vanessa noticed a girl at the house across the street. The girl, who was about her own age, started walking toward her.

"Hi, I'm Rebecca," the girl said with a friendly smile. "But my friends call me Becky. . . ."

3.11 Marcus stood in his room. He could not find his history report. He looked around the room and thought of how messy it was. No, he decided. It was more than messy. It was a disaster.

He tried to remember where he had put the report. He had finished it yesterday after school. Then he had played games online with his friends.

He looked at his desk. So many books and papers were piled on it that he could hardly see the top. He searched through each book and piece of paper. Next he searched the stuffed drawers, then he searched through the pants and shirts that lay on his dresser. He even searched under his bed, but all he found there were old sneakers.

Where was the report? He was desperate. Suddenly he remembered.

He picked up his knapsack. He had put the report in the knapsack yesterday so that he would not lose it. He looked inside, and there it was.

Hearing the horn of the school bus, Marcus grabbed his knapsack. He rushed to the door and saw the school bus driving away.

3.12 Gabriela stood in front of the big roller coaster. Anthony, her younger brother, stood beside her.

The roller coaster was called the Rocket. It was the biggest and fastest coaster Gabriela had ever seen. She had been looking forward to riding it for weeks, but now she was not sure she wanted to. Gabriela liked fast rides, but this one scared her.

"Come on, Gabriela," said Anthony. "Let's get in line." He took her hand and started pulling her toward the line of people waiting to ride the Rocket.

At first Gabriela did not move. It was as if her feet would not go. She looked at the coaster as it climbed slowly to the top of the tracks. Reaching the peak, it roared down so fast that Gabriela was certain she felt the ground shake.

"Gabriela, come on," said Anthony. "You're not afraid, are you?"

Gabriela smiled. If her little brother was not afraid, she should not be afraid either. She took a deep breath.

"Let's go," Gabriela said. She led Anthony to the line.

3.13 Ten seconds were left in the championship soccer game between the Lions and the Falcons. The score was tied 2 to 2.

Kara Johnson, the Lions' youngest player, was dribbling the ball upfield toward the Falcons' goal. Her heart was pounding, and she was tense. Kara was only in the game because Sharon Wilson, the Lions' best scorer, had been hurt earlier.

As Kara faked out a Falcon defender, she saw a small opening toward the right side of the field. She tried to keep all of her attention focused on the ball. She knew she would have only one chance for a shot.

She dodged another defender and kept moving.

"Take the shot, Kara!" she heard Sharon's voice from the sideline above the noise of the crowd.

Kara looked at the goal. The goalie was in position, staring at her. She knew she could not shoot the ball past her like this.

Kara faked a shot. She took two steps to her left to gain a better angle and kicked the ball as hard as she could.

The goalie could not stop the ball, and Kara watched the ball streak into the goal.

3.14 On a clear night, away from the lights of cities and towns, a person can see a few thousand stars. This is only a tiny part of a universe that contains billions of galaxies. Each galaxy contains billions of stars.

Stars are giant balls of burning gases made up mostly of hydrogen. Inside a star enormous pressure results in nuclear fusion. During fusion, hydrogen atoms are fused, or forced together, to make helium. Great amounts of energy are produced. It is through fusion that the heat and light of a star are created.

In recent years, astronomers have discovered that numerous stars have planets orbiting them. Our solar system no longer appears to be unique. In fact, it may be quite ordinary.

Although we do not yet have the technological capability to travel to distant stars, maybe someday we will. How wondrous it will be to find Earth-like planets in orbit around other stars. Future generations of human beings will make their homes throughout the stars.

3.15 Bears are large mammals. They have heavy bodies, short tails, and rounded ears. Although they are classified as carnivores, or meat-eaters, most bears also eat grasses, herbs, berries, nuts, and honey.

There are several kinds of bears. North American black bears, grizzly bears, and polar bears are among the most well known. North American black bears are native to North America. Black bears are one of the smallest bears and weigh between two hundred and four hundred pounds. Grizzly bears are much larger than black bears and can weigh up to a thousand pounds. Grizzlies may be brown, black, or cream-colored. The fur on their shoulders and backs is often tipped with white, giving them a "grizzled" look. Polar bears are some of the biggest bears. They may be ten feet tall and weigh up to fifteen hundred pounds. They live on the islands of the Arctic Ocean, where they hunt seals, young walruses, and fish.

In the past, bears were found throughout much of the world. Today they are found mostly in wilderness areas.

3.16 On December 16, 1811, a powerful earthquake awakened the residents of New Madrid, Missouri. This was the first of three great earthquakes and thousands of lesser aftershocks that struck the region during the winter of 1811–1812.

Many scientists are convinced that the New Madrid earthquakes were among the most powerful ever experienced in North America. The quakes were so strong that tremors were felt from Canada to Mexico and from the Rocky Mountains to the East Coast. Several towns in the region were destroyed, islands in the Mississippi River disappeared, and new lakes were formed. Eyewitness accounts of survivors reported wide cracks opening in the ground, the ground rolling in waves, and large sections of land rising and sinking. Damage from the quakes was reported as far away as Charleston, South Carolina, and Washington, DC. If such quakes occurred today in the region, the destruction would be unimaginable.

Scientists cannot predict when the next great earthquake will strike the region. Many worry that another major quake is only a matter of time.

3.17 Daniel Hale Williams (1858–1931) was an African-American physician. He performed the first successful heart surgery in 1893.

On July 9th of that year, James Cornish, a young man, was stabbed in the chest. He was brought to Provident Hospital, where Williams was a surgeon. Cornish had lost much blood, and he needed surgery to stop the bleeding. In those days internal operations almost always resulted in death from infection, but Williams knew that without surgery Cornish would die. Williams decided to operate.

During surgery, Williams found that Cornish's pericardium had been wounded. The pericardium is a sac of tissue that surrounds the heart. Williams washed the wound with a salt solution, hoping this would reduce the chance for infection. After stitching the wound, he completed the operation. James Cornish survived and lived for many more years.

Williams went on to become one of the most respected surgeons of his day. In 1913, he became the first African-American to be inducted into the American College of Surgeons.

3.18 With nervous fingers Caitlyn laced her ice skates. She took a deep breath, hoping to steady the uneasiness in her stomach.

"Don't worry," her coach said. "This time you'll do it."

That only made Caitlyn worry more. Caitlyn recalled her first attempt at completing an axel, a jump with one and a half turns in the air. She had jumped, but had fallen on her landing. Caitlyn would forever remember the sharp, knifing pain of her breaking ankle. Months passed before her ankle was fully healed.

Caitlyn had started skating again only a few weeks ago. She had not attempted an axel, but she would today.

Caitlyn stood, stepped onto the ice, and began skating. Her heart was thumping.
"You can do it," her coach said.

Caitlyn nodded and forced a weak smile.

She skated around the rink, trying to build up her courage.

Gaining speed, she knew it was now or never. She pushed off the ice, propelled herself into the air, and spun.

Her landing was perfect.

3.19 Arctic terns are small seabirds, but they are champion travelers. They make the longest migration of any bird.

Each year Arctic terns fly from the Arctic to Antarctica, only to return to the Arctic. The total distance is nearly twenty-two thousand miles, approximately the circumference of the Earth.

The terns spend the northern summers in the Arctic tundra, where they breed and make their nests. As the northern winter approaches, the terns begin flying southward until they reach the edge of the Antarctic ice pack. Because the seasons of the northern and southern hemispheres are reversed, it is now summer in Antarctica. Once summer in Antarctica ends, the terns begin flying northward again and return to the Arctic.

Arctic terns are well adapted for their long journeys. They are only twelve to fifteen inches long and weigh less than a pound. They have strong wings and streamlined bodies. They eat small fish, shrimp, and krill, which they catch by swooping down into the water.

Arctic terns have a life span of about twenty years. They spend much of their lives flying.

3.20 The ancient Olympic Games were played in Greece in the wooded valley of Olympia. Beginning in 776 B.C. and continuing until A.D. 393, they were held every four years.

No one knows who organized the first games. According to myth, Hercules, a legendary hero known throughout Greece, started the games. But the poet Pindar, in a poem he wrote in the fifth century B.C., claimed a warrior named Pelops created the games to celebrate a great victory.

The first Olympics were rather small. Only one event was held. This was the stade, a footrace of about two hundred yards. In time, a forty-thousand-seat stadium was built, and more races, wrestling, chariot racing, and the pentathlon were added. The pentathlon was a five-part event that included running, wrestling, jumping, and throwing the discus and javelin.

The Olympics were enormously popular. People from all over Greece came to watch the games. In times of war, truces were called to allow athletes and spectators to travel to Olympia safely. It is upon this grand tradition that the modern Olympic Games are founded.

3.21 When you see a bird, you are looking at a descendant of a dinosaur. Many scientists are now convinced that birds are directly related to the dinosaurs that walked the Earth millions of years ago.

The evidence for the dinosaur–bird link is strong. Just like modern birds, many dinosaurs walked on their hind legs, they had three forward-pointing toes, and they had long tails. In the 1990s, paleontologists found fossils of dinosaurs in northeastern China that had evidence of feathers. Soon more fossilized skeletons of dinosaurs were found that showed evidence of feathers and other birdlike features.

The best evidence came in 2000. Paleontologists found the fossil of a small dinosaur that they named *Microraptor zhaoianus*. It was about the size of a crow and closely resembled a bird.

Despite the evidence of birdlike features, most scientists do not consider these dinosaurs to be true birds. It is more likely these creatures are a link between dinosaurs and birds.

The dinosaurs are extinct, but their descendants are alive and well.

3.22 The Maya were among the most advanced native civilizations of the Americas. Starting around 2600 B.C., the Maya slowly gained power and influence. They came to control much of the land that is now southern Mexico, Guatemala, Belize, and Honduras.

From about A.D. 200 through 900, their society was among the most advanced in the world. The Maya constructed great cities, magnificent buildings, and pyramids that served as temples. They developed hieroglyphic writing and an accurate calendar. Mayan astronomers recorded the movements of the sun, planets, and stars.

Around 900, the Maya started to decline. No one knows why. Some historians believe wars, disease, and crop failures over a period of years might have caused the decline. This much is known. Cities in southern areas were abandoned, and the cities of the north were overcome by an invading group known as the Toltecs.

When the Spanish arrived in the sixteenth century, only a few Mayan cities remained. The great civilization was gone.

3.23 On Saturday morning Darien woke up much earlier than he usually did. He had much to do.

After a quick breakfast of cereal, milk, and juice, Darien rode his bike to soccer practice. He was the goalie for his team. He liked soccer and had been playing soccer since first grade.

After lunch, Darien helped his father with work around the house. They planted five new shrubs on the side of the house. As his father watered the shrubs, Darien weeded the flower beds. After they finished the yard work, they cleaned the garage for the rest of the afternoon.

After dinner, Darien's friends, Peter and Ricky, came over. The boys decided to play video games. They played several games, and the evening passed quickly.

By the time his friends went home, Darien was exhausted. As he went to bed, Darien thought of all the things he had to do tomorrow.

3.24 Kangaroos are found in Australia and on nearby islands. Most people are not aware that there are about a hundred different species, or kinds, of kangaroos. They range from the tiny kangaroo rat to the giant kangaroo.

The giant kangaroo, also called the great gray kangaroo, is one of the best-known species of kangaroo. Giant kangaroos stand about five feet tall and weigh up to 150 pounds. They have sheeplike heads, big ears, short front legs, long tails, and large, powerful hind legs. With its powerful legs, a giant kangaroo can jump thirty feet in a single hop and reach speeds of up to forty miles per hour.

Kangaroos are marsupials. Like other female marsupials, female kangaroos carry their young in pouches. A female kangaroo carries her young one, called a joey, in her pouch until it is old enough to survive on its own.

Kangaroos are timid creatures, but when attacked, they can be dangerous. They will use their forepaws to "punch" an attacker. They will also use their hind legs to kick and slash. A large kangaroo can seriously injure a person.

3.25 In ancient Greek mythology, Phaeton was the son of Apollo, the god of the sun. One day Phaeton went to his father's magnificent palace of the sun. Apollo was so pleased to see his son that he promised to grant Phaeton anything he asked.

Phaeton had one desire. He wanted to drive Apollo's chariot of the sun across the sky.

Apollo knew this could not be. He warned his son that no one else—not even the other gods—could drive the chariot of the sun.

Phaeton would not be swayed from his demand, and Apollo reluctantly agreed.

Phaeton climbed into the chariot and whipped the horses. The mighty animals galloped into the sky, pulling the bright sun behind the chariot. But Phaeton quickly lost control of them. They ran low to the Earth, and the blazing sun burned the ground and all on it.

When Zeus, king of the gods, realized Earth was being destroyed, he hurled a lightning bolt at Phaeton. The boy was killed, and the Earth was saved.

From that day on, all understood that only Apollo could drive the sun's chariot across the sky. They knew that a person should not try to seize control of natural forces.

Part 4

In a few articles and stories, corrections may vary depending on context. This is particularly true in the case of commas. In these cases, accept reasonable corrections. Corrected articles and stories follow.

4.1 If you have ever been caught in a thunderstorm, you may have been frightened by the lightning and thunder. Have you ever wondered what causes lightning and thunder?

The air within a thunderstorm is turbulent. As warm air rises and cool air falls, water droplets and ice crystals crash into each other. These collisions cause electrical charges to build up. Positive charges collect in the upper parts of the clouds, and negative charges collect in the lower parts. To balance the negative charges, positive charges also collect near the ground. As this process continues, the charges increase in strength. Because unlike charges attract, electricity may jump from one cloud to another or between a cloud and the ground. We see this as lightning.

A lightning bolt is extremely hot. It heats air molecules and causes them to expand violently. This causes a powerful vibration that we hear as thunder.

Thunder can be loud and frightening, but lightning is dangerous. When a thunderstorm approaches, you should seek shelter indoors. Stay away from windows and doors, and do not use electrical equipment. If you are outside, never stand near a tree. Trees can attract lightning. A lightning strike can be fatal.

4.2 Many students do not know how to study for tests. Are you one of them? If you think you are, the following tips can help.

Preparation for any test begins long before the day of the test. Keep up with your daily work and take accurate notes. On the days leading up to the test, listen to any reviews your teacher gives. This will help you to identify what may be on the test. This in turn will help you to study the right material. If you have any questions about any of the material, ask your teacher.

A day or two before the test, you should go over your notes and key parts of your textbook. Do not wait until the last minute to study. Students who study ahead of time usually do better than those who cram at the last minute.

Get a good night's sleep before the test, wake up on time, and eat a solid breakfast. Take the test with confidence. If you have studied effectively, you are likely to do well.

4.3 Martina woke up early on Thanksgiving morning. Anxious to start the day, she dressed quickly and scampered downstairs.

She found her mother in the kitchen preparing food to take to Martina's grandmother's house. That was where the entire family gathered every Thanksgiving for dinner. All of Martina's uncles, aunts, and cousins would be there.

After breakfast, Martina helped her mother pack food in a big cooler. They packed salad, fresh vegetables, fruits, and two cream pies.

Martina's grandmother lived about three hours away, and the drive seemed to take forever. As they drove, Martina wondered how many family members had already arrived. When Martina's father pulled into the driveway, she saw several cars.

Martina smiled. Everyone was here. Having Thanksgiving with the family was always a wonderful time.

4.4 Frogs are interesting creatures. They go through metamorphosis, a complete change in structure during their lives. They begin life as a fishlike tadpole and grow into a frog.

Tadpoles hatch from eggs. They breathe with gills, have streamlined bodies, and have tails. They feed on algae and tiny vegetation.

As a tadpole matures, its gills disappear, lungs develop, and legs start to grow. In time the tadpole starts eating insects and larger plant matter.

After about nine weeks of life, the tadpole looks more like a frog with a tail than a tadpole. Eventually the tail is absorbed into the tadpole's body. By about the fourth month of its life, a tadpole has made the transition to a frog. Metamorphosis is finished.

The cycle is now ready to repeat. Female frogs lay their eggs in water, from which a new generation of tadpoles hatches.

4.5 Madam C. J. Walker (1867–1919) was the most successful African-American businesswoman of the early twentieth century. She became the first African-American woman millionaire.

Madam Walker, whose birth name was Sarah Breedlove, built a company that sold hair products for African-American women. To help the company grow, Madam Walker tirelessly promoted her products. By 1910, her company had become so successful that she was able to put others in charge of the day-to-day operations. This allowed her to devote more time to lecture on issues that affected African-Americans. In her later years, Madam Walker supported numerous African-American schools, charities, and organizations.

When Madam Walker died at the age of fifty-one, she was thought to be the wealthiest African-American woman in the United States. Her life was an inspiration to women throughout the country.

4.6 Samantha hurried down the empty hallway toward her classroom. School had ended an hour ago, and she hoped her classroom was not locked. She needed to get her science book, which she had forgotten to take home. Without the book, she wouldn't be able to study for the big science test tomorrow.

Science was a difficult subject for Samantha. She had to study more for science than for any other subject.

When she got to her classroom, Samantha was relieved to find the door open. She went inside, expecting to see Mrs. Talbot, her teacher, but the room was empty. Samantha figured that Mrs. Talbot had gone home for the day.

As Samantha walked by the teacher's desk, she noticed a paper on it. Her eyes widened. It was the answer key to the test. The key could help her get a good grade.

Samantha stood there for a long moment. Taking the answers would be cheating, and that was wrong.

She went to her desk, got her science book, and left the room.

4.7 People have dreamed about flying for thousands of years. Early ideas ranged from mechanical wings that could enable a person to fly like a bird to strange machines with flapping blades. None, of course, worked.

As time passed, people looked for other ways to fly. A breakthrough came in France in 1782.

Joseph and Jacques Montgolfier, two brothers, were interested in flying. While sitting by a fireplace, Joseph filled a paper bag with smoke and hot air. As the brothers watched the bag float up to the ceiling, they got an idea.

The Montgolfiers began to experiment. They made balloons out of paper and linen and filled them with hot air from a fire. When they released the balloons, the balloons rose. The brothers built bigger and bigger balloons until they built one able to carry people.

Finally, in November of 1783, two people flew in a Montgolfier balloon. This first flight lasted twenty-five minutes and covered about five miles. The dream of flight became a reality.

4.8 Earthquakes may best be described as a shaking of the Earth. Thousands of earthquakes occur each year, but only one out of five is strong enough to be felt. On average, of every thousand earthquakes only two cause damage.

Earthquakes are caused by movement of the Earth's crust. The Earth's crust, which is its outer layer, is divided into great pieces. These pieces, called plates, are made of rock. The plates move slowly in different directions. They may grind past each other, away from each other, or toward each other. Sometimes a long crack, called a fault, forms between plates. The famous San Andreas Fault in California is a result of two plates grinding past each other. If enough stress builds up along a fault, an earthquake occurs.

Minor earthquakes cause little damage and few injuries. Major quakes can destroy entire cities and result in thousands of deaths.

4.9 It was the biggest regional track meet of the season. Andrew stretched and tried to shake the nervous tension from his body. So far this year he had won all of the two-mile races he had entered, but now he was facing boys who might be faster and have greater endurance.

The official called the boys to the starting line. Andrew took a deep breath and stepped forward.

"Remember, Andrew," Coach Simmons said, "pace yourself. Make sure you're strong for the end."

Andrew nodded. He took his position on the inside lane. He thought about his coach's advice. Andrew sometimes made the mistake of running too hard in the first part of a race. When he did that, he would fade at the end.

"On your mark!" said the official. "Get set! Go!"

The race began.

Andrew was in the middle of the pack of runners, his strides long and easy. It was a long way to the end of the race. He would make sure he was strong for the finish.

4.10

123 River Drive
Green Valley, NJ 00000
Oct. 25, 2007

Ms. Janice Williams, Circulation Manager
Extreme Skateboarding Magazine
50 Reynolds Street
Mountain Lake, CA 00000

Dear Ms. Williams:

I would like to subscribe to *Extreme Skateboarding Magazine*. Enclosed is a check for $24.95 for a subscription for one year.
Thank you.

Sincerely yours,
Thomas Jackson

4.11 Richie and I are best friends. We've been best friends for about as long as I can remember.

Some kids think it's strange that a girl and boy in seventh grade are best friends. But I don't think it's strange at all. Richie and I have a lot in common.

We've always lived next door to each other. We both like sports, we like the same type of music, and we like the same kinds of movies. But most important, we just like hanging out together. There's never any trouble between Richie and me. We stick up for each other, and we're always honest with each other. Richie's easy to talk to, and he's always willing to help when I have a problem. I do the same for him.

No matter what happens, I know I can depend on Richie, and he knows he can depend on me. I suppose that, most of all, is what makes our friendship so special.

4.12 What happened to Amelia Earhart? People have been trying to answer this question since 1937. That was the year Earhart and Fred J. Noonan, her copilot, disappeared in their plane near Howland Island in the South Pacific.

Amelia Earhart loved to fly. She became famous in May of 1932 when she made a solo flight across the Atlantic Ocean. She followed this feat with several solo long-distance flights across the U.S. In January of 1931, she made a solo flight from Hawaii to California.

Earhart attempted her most daring flight in June of 1937. With copilot Noonan, she set off to make an around-the-world flight. On July 2nd their plane vanished. Rescue teams mounted extensive search efforts, but no sign of Earhart, Noonan, or their plane was ever found.

In the following years, researchers and mystery buffs have tried to discover what happened to Amelia Earhart. None have succeeded, and Amelia Earhart's disappearance remains a mystery.

4.13 Giorgio stared at the overcast sky. He turned to Danny, his friend.

"It looks like rain," Giorgio said.

"According to the weather forecast," said Danny, "there's only a slight chance of showers."

The two boys had just arrived at the baseball field for the first game of the season. Some of the players of both teams were already there.

Coach Bennett instructed the boys to begin warming up.

Giorgio and Danny took their places with their teammates and began playing catch.

Giorgio looked back at the sky. Baseball was his favorite sport, and he had been looking forward to this first game for weeks.

"Giorgio, quit worrying," said Danny. "The game will start on time."

"I hope so," said Giorgio.

A little while later, the sun poked through the clouds.

"See," said Danny. "The sun's coming out. Now you'll be worrying about the sun getting into your eyes."

Giorgio smiled. "You're probably right."

4.14 Step into my house, and you will find books and magazines everywhere. Everybody in my family enjoys reading. We read for entertainment and information.

My father rides the bus to work each morning. During his commute he reads *The New York Times*. He also reads magazines. His favorites are *Time* and *Discover*.

My mother enjoys reading novels. She reads a new novel every week. She likes mysteries the best, but she also likes romances. Sometimes she likes a book so much that she can't put it down until she finishes it.

Jessica, my older sister, likes short stories and poems. One of her favorite short stories is "The Dinner Party" by Mona Gardner. Her favorite poem is Lewis Carroll's "Jabberwocky."

As for me, I mostly read novels. My favorites are fantasies with heroes, evil villains, and magic. If I had to pick one favorite, I would choose *The Hobbit* by J. R. R. Tolkien.

4.15 Emily stuck her ski poles into the snow to steady herself. She stood on the top of the mountain and looked down the slope. Daredevil Trail disappeared in the distance.

She felt a gentle pat on her shoulder.

"You can make it down," said Alyssa, her big sister.

"That's not what worries me," said Emily. She forced a smile. "I'm worried about how many broken bones I'll have."

"You don't have to do this," Alyssa said.

"Yes, I do," said Emily, who prided herself on her skill at skiing. "This is the only trail on this mountain I've never gone down."

Alyssa smiled. "You'll be fine," she said. "Keep your knees bent and remember to lean into the turns."

Emily nodded. "Here I go." She pushed off with her poles and started down the trail.

She heard Alyssa's voice behind her.

"You can do it."

As Emily leaned into the first turn, she hoped her sister was right.

4.16 The sounds of laughter, the honking of a car horn, and the roar of a lawn mower's motor are all produced in the same way. But do you know how those sounds are produced?

All sounds are a result of vibrations. When something vibrates, it moves back and forth rapidly. Imagine plucking a string on a violin. As the string vibrates, it makes a sound. Of course, you seldom see the vibrations that cause sound, because the vibrations are too small and are moving too fast. Unlike plucking a string, imagine tapping a pencil on a desk. You can't see the vibrations, but you hear the sound of the tapping.

When an object vibrates, it causes the nearby molecules in the air to move. As the molecules move, the vibrations travel through the air in the form of waves. Like the ripples that result from a stone tossed in a pond, the waves move outward from the point of the sound in every direction. When these waves reach your ear, you hear the sound.

As sound waves move outward from a vibrating object, they become weaker. This is why a sound becomes fainter the farther away you are from its source.

4.17 Have you ever played chess? If you have, you have played a game that has been around for at least fifteen hundred years.

Chess is a game of skill and strategy played by two players. The game is based on the warfare of the Middle Ages. Each player has sixteen pieces that he plays on a square board. The board is divided into sixty-four alternate light and dark squares. When a player lands a piece on a space occupied by one of his opponent's pieces, that piece is removed from the board. The object of the game is to capture, or checkmate, the opponent's king. Capture of the king ends the game.

No one knows who invented chess. Most historians believe the game originated in India about the sixth century A.D. The game slowly spread westward through Persia (modern Iran) and reached Europe sometime between 700 and 900.

The modern game began to evolve during the sixteenth and seventeenth centuries. Today, chess is played around the world and is as popular as ever.

4.18 A volcano is a mountain with a vent, or opening, to the interior of the Earth. Magma (hot, melted rock) from inside the Earth passes through the vent to the surface. Sometimes the magma flows out slowly, but sometimes it erupts in great explosions.

Volcanoes can be in one of three states: active, dormant, or extinct. An active volcano is erupting or shows signs of erupting soon. A dormant volcano has not erupted in some time but may erupt again in the future. An extinct volcano is no longer capable of erupting.

Volcanic eruptions start far beneath the surface. When magma comes under great pressure, it rises through cracks and weak spots in the rock. Eventually the magma finds its way to the surface. If the pressure is intense, the magma may erupt. Along with magma, eruptions usually include gases, ash, and steam.

Magma that flows out of a volcano is called lava. Lava can reach temperatures of 2,000 degrees Fahrenheit or more. Flowing down a volcano's sides, lava can destroy everything in its path.

Scientists study volcanoes in the hope of learning how to predict eruptions. Such knowledge would help them warn people before an eruption occurs.

4.19 Brianna stepped from the dock and into the boat. She plopped onto the nearest seat. She was not happy being here. She and her parents were about to spend one of their vacation days in search of whales. Brianna would have preferred to spend the day at the oceanside resort where the family was staying for the week.

"I've been looking forward to today for months," Brianna's mother said.

"I haven't," Brianna said. "I'd rather be at the beach."

"You can go to the beach every day for the rest of our vacation," said her father. "But if we're lucky, today you can see a whale."

Brianna didn't like boats, and she liked the idea of searching for whales even less. As the boat left the dock, Brianna sighed. This was going to be a long day.

It was early afternoon when the captain directed everyone to look ahead.

"There!" cried one of the passengers.

Brianna looked and saw a magnificent animal rise from the water.

"It's incredible," she said, suddenly glad she was here and not back on the beach.

4.20 One of the most wonderful features of the world is color. Colors help to make things distinct. Just think of a blue sky, a red rose, or the pure whiteness of freshly fallen snow. Can you imagine how dull the world would be without color?

The basics of colors are surprisingly simple. Colors can be divided into three kinds: primary, secondary, and intermediate. The primary colors are red, yellow, and blue. They can't be made by mixing any other colors. The secondary colors, which are made by mixing two primary colors, are orange, green, and violet. Mixing red and yellow makes orange. Mixing yellow and blue makes green. Mixing blue and red makes violet. Intermediate colors are made by mixing primary and secondary colors. Mixing white or black with colors will make them lighter or darker.

It's remarkable that all colors are based on combinations of red, yellow, and blue. The world truly is a colorful place.

4.21 I was upstairs working on my book report when Marlena, my little sister, called me from downstairs.

"Come quick, Angela!" she cried.

"What's wrong?" I said, getting up from my desk and hurrying to the stairs.

"It's Puffin!" Marlena said. "She's in a big tree. She can't get down." Puffin was our cat.

I hurried downstairs and followed Marlena out the front door.

Looking up at the big oak tree in our yard, I saw Puffin sitting on a high branch. She had climbed up, but she was afraid to climb down.

"Puffin, come down right now," I said. A mournful meow was my answer.

There wasn't anything I could do except to keep calling Puffin down. But the cat wouldn't budge.

I was glad when my father came home from work. He got a ladder, climbed up, and got Puffin.

I smiled as Marlena scolded the foolish cat.

"Puffin, I never want you to climb that tree again," she said.

4.22 If you have ever seen a rainbow in the sky, you have witnessed one of the beauties of nature. The typical rainbow makes an arc in the sky. Sometimes a rainbow is so big that its ends seem to touch the Earth.

The mystery of a rainbow lies in sunlight and water droplets. A ray of sunlight contains all the colors of the spectrum: red, orange, yellow, green, blue, and violet. When sunlight shines through water droplets, the droplets separate the sunlight into its different colors. Under the right conditions this creates a rainbow.

Rainbows may appear anywhere sunlight shines on water droplets, but they most often are seen near the end of a rain shower. They may also appear in the spray of a waterfall, a fountain, or a garden hose.

According to legend, a pot of gold awaits you at the end of a rainbow. Of course, you can never reach the end. As you approach a rainbow, the rainbow seems to retreat and soon disappears.

4.23 Dawn walked up the steps to the home of Mr. and Mrs. Ross and rang the doorbell. This was the first time she was to babysit for Matthew, their son. She hoped Matthew, who was only five years old, would behave. Christina, Dawn's best friend, babysat for Matthew once, and she vowed never to babysit for him again.

Mrs. Ross opened the door and greeted Dawn with a friendly smile.

Dawn saw Matthew standing in the living room. He was smiling too. He seemed like a nice boy.

After Mrs. Ross gave Dawn instructions, she and her husband got ready to leave.

"Remember, Dawn," Mrs. Ross said at the door, "Matthew must be in bed no later than nine o'clock."

"I'll remember," Dawn said.

For the next two hours Dawn read to Matthew, they drew and colored, and they watched Matthew's favorite video. Matthew was so pleasant that Dawn began to wonder if Christina had babysat for the same boy.

At nine o'clock Dawn told Matthew that it was time for bed.

Matthew looked at her and smiled.

"No!" he said firmly. "And you can't make me go to bed."

Dawn thought of Christina and realized that it was going to be a long night.

4.24 It was the final day of wrestling camp. Dan was to wrestle Brett in the championship match for their weight class.

Dan looked at Brett and frowned. He doubted that he could defeat Brett. Brett was a year older and had more experience.

"Brett's a great wrestler," Dan said to Roberto, his best friend.

"He is," said Roberto, "but he loses his cool. He likes to pin his opponents fast. But when that doesn't happen, he gets mad and makes mistakes."

"But how does that help me?" said Dan. "He's faster and stronger than I am."

"You have to wrestle smart," said Roberto. "Don't let him gain the advantage. He'll get frustrated and then you make your move."

"You mean stay on defense until he makes a mistake," said Dan.

Roberto nodded.

Soon after the match began, Dan realized his friend was right. When the match was finished, Dan was a wrestling champion.

4.25 Commander Sarto stood on the bridge of his starship and watched the main viewing screen. As they approached the tiny planet, it grew on the screen. Sarto studied the oceans and land masses that appeared through the clouds. The planet reminded him of home.

"Take us into orbit," he said to Jartan, his second in command. "Then see if you can listen to their communications."

Sarto thought of his mission to make contact with the beings that lived on the planet. He wondered what they were like.

He noticed the concern that had come to Jartan's face.

"What's the matter?" Sarto said.

"There must be some mistake," said Jartan. "The transmissions I'm picking up indicate that these beings are quite violent. They're not ready to join the United Planets."

Sarto sighed. He had seen this happen before.

"Sometimes the first survey teams make errors in their evaluations," Sarto said. "Set course for the next planet. Make a note to visit Earth again in about a hundred years."